Artistic Pedal Technique

Lessons for Intermediate and Advanced Pianists

Katherine Faricy

3rd edition
Published by **MaryMarkMusic** © 2018 Minnetonka, MN

PREFACE

My awareness of the importance of thoughtful pedaling and its myriad possibilities began in graduate school where I learned about the principle of ten levels of pedal as taught by the famed Russian pianist Rosina Lhévinne. When I began teaching college students, I realized that my students were no more knowledgeable about pedaling than I had been in my early training. Convinced that a methodical approach to teaching this area of pianism was important, I looked for some helpful teaching materials but they weren't to be found. I therefore created the exercises and notation that became the basis of this volume. I have found this approach extremely effective in helping my students develop a thoughtful and artistic pedal technique.

I owe thanks to many people for their help in bringing this volume into being. First of all, I wish to thank my dear friend and colleague Seymour Bernstein for his valuable advice, encouragement, and support. In addition, there were so many others who helped me along the way that I cannot name them all. But I would like to give special thanks to the following colleagues and friends for the generous time and expertise they gave to the manuscript and the many revisions: James Callahan, Beatriz Aguerrevere, Jon Iverson, Ann Cader, Carol Flatou. Last but not least I thank my students for their inspiration and all I learned from them.

Katherine Faricy
Minnetonka, Minnesota
2018

Katherine Faricy graduated from the Oberlin College Conservatory of Music with a bachelor's degree in music education and received her master of fine arts degree in piano performance from the University of Minnesota. She also studied privately for four years with the renowned concert pianist, Madame Lili Kraus. As a member of the faculty at the University of St. Thomas in St. Paul, Minnesota, she taught undergraduate piano, piano ensemble, accompanying, and music literature; as well as graduate piano and courses in performance practices, piano literature, and piano pedagogy. A frequent recitalist and soloist with orchestras, Katherine Faricy serves as an adjudicator and clinician. It was during studies with Kraus she became very aware of the importance of pedaling in artistic performance and how few people are taught its technique. *Artistic Pedal Technique—Lessons for Intermediate and Advanced Pianists* was first published in 2004 and has become an international success. In 2009 Faricy's newest book was published, *Pedaling~Colors in Sound; Lessons and Repertoire for Elementary Students*.

CONTENTS

INTRODUCTION

Purpose and organization

Chopin said, "To learn to use the pedal correctly is a lifelong study." Anton Rubinstein said, "The longer I play, the more convinced I am that the pedal is the soul of the piano. There are places where the pedal means everything."[1] Artistic and correct pedaling is necessary for truly successful interpretation; bad pedaling can ruin an otherwise satisfactory performance.

This book is intended to provide pianists with an organized approach to developing the control necessary for artistic pedaling and to acquaint them with the myriad ways of creating desired pedal effects.

Artistic Pedal Technique provides teachers and students with specific exercises to acquire control of the pedals and foster careful listening, and introduces techniques that can be used in a variety of repertoire and styles. The pedal indications for the music examples are merely suggestions, showing the pedaling that could be used in such situations.

The units on each of the pedals include background information, exercises, repertoire examples, and suggestions for appropriate uses. The most extensive unit, Unit One—The Damper Pedal, is further divided into eleven lessons on the numerous uses of the damper pedal. Teachers and students should refer to Unit Four—Stylistic Principles of Pedaling when studying the repertoire examples in each lesson. The material in the lessons will give teachers and students a systematic and progressive procedure for developing artistic pedal technique.

Pedagogy of pedaling

Technique of the feet must be taught as carefully and methodically as technique of the hands. Pedal technique, however, is the least understood and most neglected area of piano pedagogy. There are understandable reasons for this neglect.

- The use of the pedals is often not notated by composers, and when it is, the notation for pedaling is often confusing, imprecise, or even inaccurate.
- The use of the pedals is dependent upon variables such as the instrument, the acoustics of the room, and especially what the pianist does with articulation and dynamics.
- Few teachers have been taught pedal technique. Students are therefore often left to their own intuitive reactions. Possibly, the only instructions are where *not* to pedal, with the thought that no pedaling is better than poor pedaling.
- There have been few pedaling method books written to help students develop proficient pedal technique, and most of them are out of print. With few exceptions, these books discuss pedaling without providing technical exercises necessary to achieve the desired results.

Proper position for pedaling

1. Sit on the front third of the piano bench so that your weight is equally distributed between your seat and the heels of your feet. Your torso should be balanced on the "sitz" bones (ischial tuberosity); no part of the thighs should be supported by the bench.
2. Place your feet on the left and right pedals (soft or *una corda* pedal and damper pedal respectively). The balls of the feet (where they connect to the toes) should be in contact with the surface of the pedals. The heels must be directly aligned behind the toes in a straight line. It is important to keep the knees relaxed. Do not squeeze them together, as doing so puts a strain on the hip joints.

---

[1] Reimer Riefling, *Piano Pedaling*. Trans. Kathleen Dale. London: Oxford University Press, 1962, p. 1.

3. Keep the feet on both the damper and soft pedals at all times, regardless how much or how little you intend to use the pedals in a piece. Many pianists are in the habit of keeping the left foot on the floor or under the bench for support, but that position does not invite the use of the soft pedal. If you are seated properly with an elongated spine balanced on the "sitz" bones, your heels will provide the necessary support.

Although there are occasions when you need to bring the left foot back to the floor to help support the body, such as in loud or very active passages, these occasions are rare and should be exceptions. Keeping the feet on the pedals allows for the brief and occasional applications that are part of an artistic performance. If the feet are on the floor, a pianist is not likely to bother with a momentary application. Also, many a beautiful *pianissimo* passage has been ruined by the disruption of the left foot being brought from the floor to the soft pedal at the last moment, just when the greatest quiet is intended. Occasionally, a last-minute positioning of the foot results in the foot ending up on the wrong pedal—with catastrophic results!

Admittedly, there is some controversy about keeping the foot on the soft pedal, but almost all concert artists sit as suggested here, and the author's own training, teaching, and performing experience supports the stated logic for doing so.

Keeping the ball of the foot in contact with the pedal:
- allows for careful control of release of the pedal without the percussive noise that occurs when the pedal is let go suddenly and springs back to the top of its own accord;
- prevents noisy tapping of the shoe during application of the pedal;
- ensures that the pedal is actually engaged in short, shallow pedal applications.

It is important to wear proper shoes when playing the piano. The shoe sole should be firm enough to provide support but thin enough for the foot to feel the pedal. High heels restrict the range of motion and can create shin strain. Playing without shoes leads to cramping of the foot.

Practice suggestions

1. Concentrate on listening intently to all exercises and repertoire. The most important element in learning to pedal is the development of an acute ear.

2. Do not distract the ear by counting aloud or by using the metronome while playing. Stay focused on the sound of the piano.

3. All pianists, regardless of level of ability, should work through all of the exercises at their own pace. Do not begin a new exercise until you have mastered the one you are working on.

4. Pianists who are capable of playing the more advanced repertoire examples in this book should first work through all of the intermediate examples in each lesson. Intermediate students need only work on repertoire examples that are appropriate to their level of ability. You should be secure and comfortable with each concept before you move to the next.

5. Read the text that introduces the repertoire examples carefully so you will understand the principles guiding the pedaling choices.

6. When the pedaling is complex, practice the left hand (or in some cases, the right hand) alone with pedal. After your coordination is secure, add the other hand. Be sure to apply and release the pedal precisely where indicated (or decided upon), whether playing with one hand or two.

7. As you progress through the book, go back to previous lessons to apply the new techniques to those exercises and repertoire where appropriate. For example, after perfecting Lesson 3—Syncopated Pedal at Various Depths, go back to Lesson 2 and try the different depths there.

THE DAMPER PEDAL

INTRODUCTION TO THE DAMPER PEDAL

Uses of the damper pedal

1. *To enhance the beauty of a single tone or chord*
   The warmer tone created when the damper pedal is engaged is analogous to the enrichment of tone provided by *vibrato* in string, wind, and vocal tone production. This use of the pedal is appropriate in piano literature of all historical style periods; the amount used depends on the context and style, as does the use of *vibrato* with other instruments.

2. *To sustain notes that cannot be held with fingers alone*
   The use of the damper pedal allows notes to sound together even though they cannot be struck simultaneously. Some instances include:
   • arpeggios where all notes are to continue to sound;
   • *legato* octaves and chords;
   • held bass notes in accompaniments (such as waltz accompaniments);
   • places where more notes are indicated (sometimes on three staves) than the pianist can play with just two hands.

3. *To connect repeated melody notes*

4. *To reinforce accents*

5. *To help with* crescendos

6. *To help with* diminuendos

7. *To provide a tapered ending to a tone or chord*

8. *To create blurred atmospheric effects*

9. *To enhance and emphasize phrasing and articulation*
   The tone that a pianist produces is a combination of what is done with the fingers and with the pedal. A detached note held by a pedal creates a different color than does a fingered *legato* with or without pedal. These subtleties contribute to an artistic performance.

10. *To provide color appropriate to the mood or character of the music*
    Pedaled passages, phrases, or sections provide contrast with those that are unpedaled.

The damper mechanism

A set of felt dampers rests on the piano strings, one damper for each key. When a key is depressed, the mechanism causes a hammer to strike a string while simultaneously lifting the damper; this allows the string to vibrate as long as the finger holds down the key. Because the right pedal controls the damper mechanism, it is commonly referred to as the "damper" pedal.

If the right pedal is depressed while the keys are held down, the whole set of dampers is raised, allowing all the strings to vibrate sympathetically; this enriches the tonal quality of the keys being held. When the pedal is released, the dampers return to their original position on the strings, stopping the vibrations.

Upright pianos

Sophisticated use of the pedal is more difficult on an upright piano than on a grand. Unlike a grand piano, the mechanism of an upright does not work with gravity. A pianist should have at least occasional access to a grand piano while developing an artistic pedal technique.

Regulation

The damper pedal must be regulated properly, so that the dampers will engage at the slightest pressure on the pedal. Regulation is a task best left to a competent technician.

If you hear notes ceasing to sound at slightly different times when releasing chords with the pedal alone, the dampers themselves need regulating. Although regulation can be complicated and costly, the procedure is an important one. The action, damper mechanism, and pedal mechanisms should all be well regulated.

Notation of artistic damper pedaling

One drawback of pedal notation, both old and new (see Appendix A), is that it usually does not indicate precisely where one is to depress or release the pedal. Furthermore, there is no commonly used notation that indicates the speed or depth of pedal application and release.

In this book, the pedaling to be used in the exercises and music examples is indicated with a unique notation that shows as clearly as possible the exact timing, manner, and depth of applications and releases.

The pedal is notated on a separate staff, with the top line representing the foot at rest on the pedal without engaging the damper mechanism. The bottom line represents the pedal fully depressed. The other lines represent 1/4, 1/2, and 3/4 pedal depth. Speed and timing of application and release are indicated graphically with lines.

This type of detailed pedal notation is obviously not practical in published music. Therefore, when students begin to transfer the new techniques to their own scores, they should create their own form of notation to indicate pedaling with different depths, applications, and releases, as shown in the following example:

Wolfgang Amadeus Mozart, *Sonata in C Major*, K 330, second movement

Andante cantabile

Finger-pedaling

A common technique for maintaining *legato* playing is *finger-pedaling*. With this technique, the pianist creates the effect of pedaling simply by holding down keys with the fingers. This works especially well when accompaniments need a pedaled sound while the melody has a variety of articulations requiring subtle and occasional use of the damper pedal. Finger-pedaling is sometimes indicated by double stems, but most often, the choice is left to the performer.

In this book, double stems are used to indicate finger-pedaling.

without finger-pedaling   with finger-pedaling

LESSON 1—CONTROL OF DEPTHS OF DAMPER PEDAL

Many pianists treat the damper pedal like a light switch: it is either on or off. However, for artistic pedal technique, you must think of the pedal as a dimmer (or rheostat) switch that can turn the light gradually on or off or leave it at a low, medium, or high level of intensity, or any level in between.

Technique

Artistic pedaling requires that the pianist be able to pedal at various depths, both in applications and releases. This ability is not as difficult as it may seem; even beginning students can easily develop the ability to control the pedal at four levels. An intermediate student should be able to control the damper pedal at six levels of depth, with control over the timing, manner, and depth of both application and release. Advanced students should work toward being able to pedal at ten levels of depth. Finding six to ten distinct levels of the pedal becomes possible and natural as you achieve facility and become accustomed to the feel of the pedal and the sound associated with each level.

It is important to realize that once you are aware of the damper pedal's possibilities and consciously gain the facility to control the pedal at the various levels, you will not "think" specific levels when playing repertoire. Rather, you will instinctively use the appropriate depth. Ultimately, of course, pedaling is guided by the ear.

Exercises

The following exercises are for foot and pedal only. They will help you to discover the range of the damper pedal and gain control over partial applications and releases. Learning to control the pedal with the foot alone is an important first step before trying to coordinate the foot with the hands.

In the following exercises, strive to reach the proper level immediately and precisely.
Place your foot correctly on the damper pedal as described on pp. 4–5.

Exercise 1
1. Depress the damper pedal all the way down.
2. Release the pedal all the way up without allowing the foot to lose contact with the pedal. Feel the resistance of the pedal pushing the foot up, rather than letting the pedal come up freely of its own accord.

Repeat these movements until you have a feeling for the pedal's range of motion. If you are playing a grand piano, look under the music rack at the dampers to see how they engage. If the mechanism is properly adjusted, the dampers should move at the first slight pressure of the foot. However, it is important that you learn this exercise by feeling the distance, not by looking at the dampers.

Exercise 2
1. Depress pedal 1/2 the way down, then all the way down.
2. Release pedal 1/2 the way up, then all the way up.

Repeat these steps until you are sure that you have found the exact halfway mark by feeling, not by looking. At first, it is common for pianists to go down past the halfway mark because they are used to engaging the pedal to its greatest depth.

Exercise 3
1. Depress pedal 1/4 the way down, 1/2 the way down, 3/4 the way down, then depress all the way down.
2. Release pedal 1/4 the way up, 1/2 the way up, 3/4 the way up, then all the way up.

Practice these moves until you can find the positions easily and accurately.

Exercise 4

1. Depress pedal 1/8 the way down, 1/4 the way down, 1/2 the way down, 3/4 the way down, 7/8 the way down, then all the way down.

2. Release pedal 1/8 the way up, 1/4 the way up, 1/2 the way up, 3/4 the way up, 7/8 the way up, then all the way up.

Repeat until the moves are easy and accurate.

You are now able to control the pedal at six different levels.

Exercise 5

1. Depress pedal 1/8 the way down, 1/4 the way down, 3/8 the way down, 1/2 the way down, 5/8 the way down, 3/4 the way down, 7/8 the way down, then all the way down.

2. Reverse the process (as you have been doing in the previous exercises), and practice until the moves are secure.

Exercise 6

1. Depress pedal *less than* 1/8 the way down, 1/8 the way down, 1/4 the way down, 3/8 the way down, 1/2 the way down, 5/8 the way down, 3/4 the way down, 7/8 the way down, *a little more than* 7/8 the way down, then all the way down.

2. Reverse the process and repeat until the moves are accurate and easy.

You now have the ability to control the application and release of the damper pedal at ten different levels.

LESSON 2—SYNCOPATED PEDAL

Syncopated pedaling is used in *legato* passages. It can be used to enhance the quality of sound in single-note melodies, warming the tone in the same way that *vibrato* does in the voice or other instruments. It is also used in accompanied melodies and for connecting *legato* chords. While you should not let the pedal substitute for a good finger *legato*, syncopated pedal is particularly helpful in *legato* chords that are repeated or are too far apart to connect in any other way.

Technique

Syncopated (or *legato*) pedal is a technique wherein the pedal is applied after the hand plays, and is released when the hand plays the next note or chord, as is clearly illustrated in the exercises in this lesson. It requires both precise coordination between hand and foot and careful listening to guide the timing of the application and release of the pedal. While normally this technique is used to connect one note to the next, the early release of the pedal can give a breathing space to indicate phrasing.

Exercises

- As you practice the following exercises, be sure to keep the dynamic volume at *mezzo forte* for valid comparison of the sounds produced by the different levels of pedal.
- Count silently at a steady tempo, and make sure you play the chord and depress and release the pedal precisely where indicated.
- Listen carefully to the change in the sound when the pedal is applied.
- As you release each chord, listen intently to the sound sustained by the pedal.
- Listen carefully when you play the next chord. If the pedal is released too soon, you will hear a break in the sound between chords. If the pedal is released too late, there will be a blurring of the two chords. When the timing is correct, you should hear a clean *legato* connection between the chords.

Exercise 1

1. On count 1, play the chord.
2. On count 2, depress the pedal.
3. On count 3, release the chord and listen.
4. On count 4, continue to listen to the sound retained by the pedal alone.
5. On the next count of 1, be sure to release the pedal exactly as the chord sounds.

Exercise 2

Repeat *Exercise 1*, but depress the pedal on the "and" of beat 1 instead of waiting until beat 2.

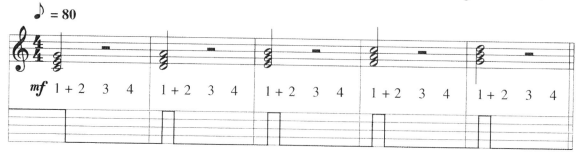

Exercise 3

Repeat *Exercise 2*, but start with the pedal depressed. This often-neglected technique can be used on the first note of a piece to create a beautiful sound with overtones.

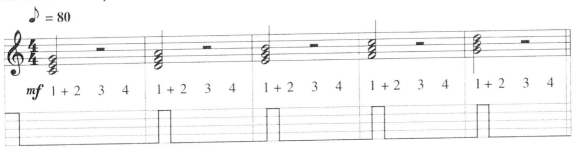

Exercise 4

Repeat *Exercise 2*, but now maintain a precise eighth-note rhythm with foot and left hand.

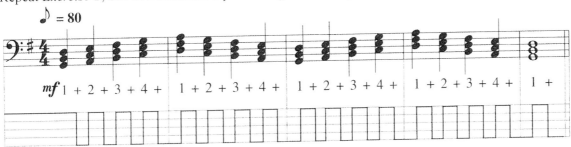

Exercise 5

Repeat *Exercise 4*, but depress the pedal earlier.

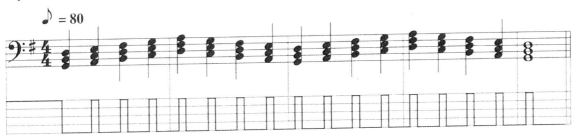

Music examples using syncopated pedal

Robert Benedict, *Shallows*

Christopher Norton, *Dreaming*

The score is marked *con pedale* (with pedal). You may pedal as indicated below, or pedal once a measure. Later in the score, longer pedals are indicated for a few measures. The pedaling suggested below for the beginning of the piece provides contrast to the later measures.

Franz Liszt, *Consolation No. 1*

Where *portato* is indicated, the chords should be played slightly separated, with sound maintained by the pedal. Be sure to play *legato* where indicated, and lift your hands at the end of slurs. Note that the pedal is to be depressed before you play. Also try depressing the pedal after the first chord and compare the effect.

Frédéric Chopin, *Prélude in C Minor,* **op. 28, no. 20**

In Baroque music, you must not catch two or more consecutive pitches of any one voice (soprano, alto, tenor, or bass) in the pedal. The purpose of using pedal in this music is to add color to the sound without sacrificing clarity. The pedaling should not be obvious to listeners.

J.S. Bach, *Prélude in B flat Minor,* **WTC, book I**

J.S. Bach, *Prélude in E flat Minor,* **WTC, book I**

LESSON 3—SYNCOPATED PEDAL AT VARIOUS DEPTHS

Listen, listen, and keep on listening. The most important element in the artistic use of the damper pedal is the development of a discerning ear. Just as visual artists must look at the canvas as they are painting, pianists must listen to the quality and quantity of sounds they create as they play. Many pianists listen for the correct notes and rhythms, but they tend to neglect listening to the sounds they make. When they listen, it is usually only to the beginning of the sound, not through its duration. They listen to what they do *to* the piano, but not to what the piano *does*.

Technique

Artistic pedal technique is dependent on the pianist's ability to pedal at different depths. The appropriate depth is determined by:
- the appropriate sound for the style and/or character of the music;
- the speed of the pedal changes;
- the dynamics;
- the desired clarity;
- the individual finger technique, the particular piano, and the acoustics of the room.

Experiment to find the sound associated with each level of pedal as described in the following exercises. Because of the differences in instruments, you should associate the different levels of the pedal with the sound, not with the physical depth of the pedal.

Exercises

These exercises using syncopated pedal technique deal with the sound associated with each of the different depths of the damper pedal.
- Listen carefully to the amount and quality of sound when the hand releases the chord. The piano sonority and the regulation of the pedal mechanism will be different on each instrument.
- Be sure that the dynamic level of the chords remains *mezzo forte*. There is a tendency when partially depressing the pedal to depress the keys only partially as well, which makes it impossible to compare the sounds associated with the different depths.
- Keep in mind that the shallower the pedal depth, the easier it is to make fast pedal changes that are clean and free from thumping sounds.

Exercise 1 – no pedal

Play one key *forte* in the middle of the keyboard with no pedal, and listen until no sound remains. Listen carefully to the way the tone blooms a bit at the beginning, and to its subtle waves of vibrations. Each piano has a different rate of decay, so listen to how quickly the decay occurs on the instrument you are playing. (Ideally, a modern piano should not have a discernible decay early in the sound.) In other words, listen to what the tone does by itself after you play a key.

Exercise 2 – full pedal

1. On count 1, play the chord.
2. On count 2, depress the pedal.
3. On count 3, release the chord and listen for any change in sound.
4. On count 4, listen for the sound retained by the pedal alone.

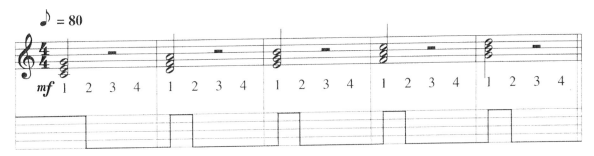

Compare this sound to that of *Exercise 1*.

Exercise 3 – 3/4 pedal

1. On count 1, play the chord.
2. On count 2, depress the pedal 3/4 the way down.
3. On count 3, release the chord and listen for any change of sound.
4. On count 4, listen to the sound retained by the pedal alone.

If you have found the 3/4 level of pedal, the sound maintained by the pedal alone will be full, with virtually no difference from a fully depressed pedal. Remember that the shallower the pedal, the smaller the risk of thumping sounds.

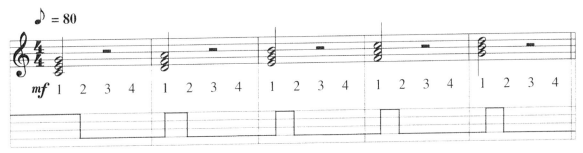

Exercise 4 – 1/2 pedal

Follow the same steps as in the previous exercises, but depress pedal 1/2 the way down. If you have accurately found the halfway level, the sound maintained by the pedal will still be full, with virtually no difference from full pedal.

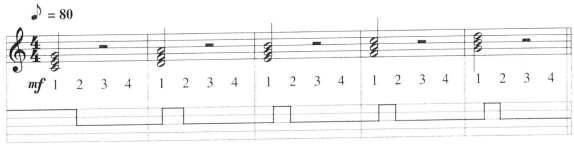

Exercise 5 – 1/4 pedal

Depress the pedal only 1/4 the way down. When the chord is released, you should hear the "edges" of the sound "shrink" a bit (as it can best be described), but the sound will still be substantially full. Be sure to associate all pedal depths with their sound, not with the physical depth of the pedal.

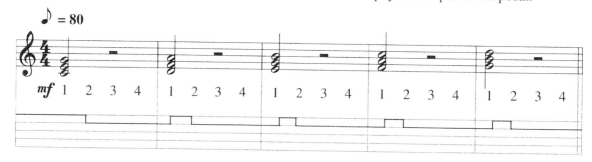

Exercise 6 – 1/8 pedal

When the chord is released, you should hear most of the sound "shrink," although the chord should still be wholly audible. (If one note or another does not sound at release, even though all notes were even in tone when played, the cause is likely poorly adjusted dampers.)

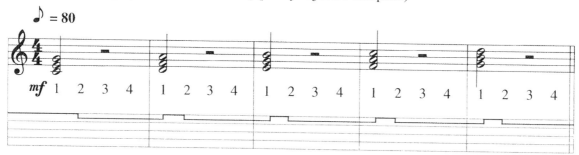

Exercise 7 – less than 1/8 pedal

When the chord is released, there should be just a slight haze of sound, like smoke in the air.

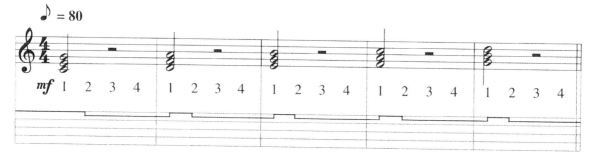

Exercise 8 – waltz bass for left hand

Be sure to catch the bass note with the pedal. Experiment with different depths.

Exercise 9
Try this waltz bass with different timings of release.

Music examples using different depths and timings of application and release

Johannes Brahms, *Waltz in G sharp Minor*, **op. 39, no. 3**
The shallower pedals are appropriate for the *piano dolce* marking, and the deeper pedals for the *crescendos*.

Franz Schubert, *Sentimental Waltz,* op. 50, no. 13

In these excerpts, the timing of applications and releases supports the syncopations and the Viennese waltz style, which has a lift on the second beat. The shallower pedals help to maintain the *piano* dynamic and the slender tone associated with Schubert's piano.

Practice first with left hand and pedal only, then add the right hand.

(a)

(b)

Larysa Kuzmenko, *Romance*

Here too, the depth of pedal is related to the dynamics; the shallower pedals allow for smoother, quick changes of pedal. The score is marked *con pedale*, which allows for choice of pedaling by the performer. The element of counterpoint in the left hand and the non-harmonic tones suggest changing pedals rather than pedaling once a measure. However, in the places where the left-hand part is more harmonic, longer pedals are more appropriate.

Practice left hand and pedal together before adding the right hand.

Frédéric Chopin, *Prélude in E Minor*, **op. 28, no. 4**
Here, the pedal changes with the changes of harmony, not just with the melody notes. Pedal depths are related to dynamics.

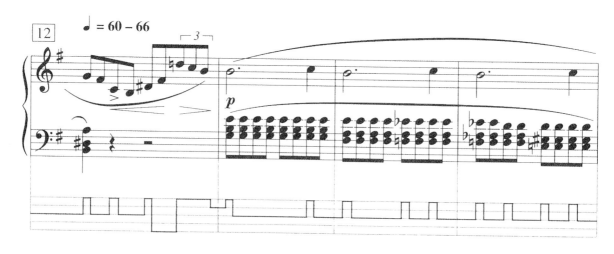

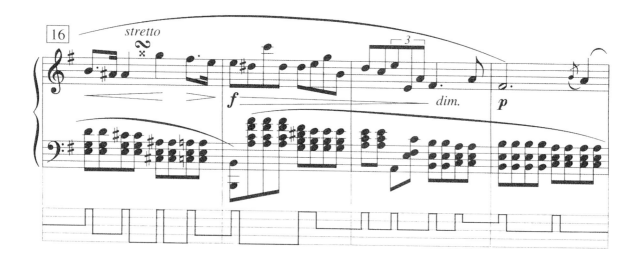

Frédéric Chopin, *Prélude in B Minor*, op. 28, no. 6

Pedal for the melody in the left hand, maintaining clarity while keeping the right-hand accompaniment *legato*. Different depths of pedal enhance the subtle dynamic shapes.

Franz Schubert, *Impromptu in B flat Major*, op. 142, no. 3
Note how the differing depths of application and release of the pedal support the dynamics and the clarity of sound associated with Schubert's style. (Articulation in mm. 1–2 continues throughout.)

Wolfgang Amadeus Mozart, *Fantasie in C Minor*, K 475

This is another example of how pedaling can enhance the dynamics and create the slender tone appropriate for Mozart's music. Note that in mm. 6–8, finger-pedaling the left hand, as indicated below, allows you to pedal the melody notes without muddying the texture.

Robert Schumann, *Papillons*, op. 2, no. 1

A shallow pedal assists with the *legato* octaves while keeping the soft dynamic and clarity of texture.
You can also hear the influence of the pedal on the character of the music and rhythmic accents in
mm. 9–12.

In mm. 12–14, the pedal marks are from Schumann's notation, so a long pedal is called for.

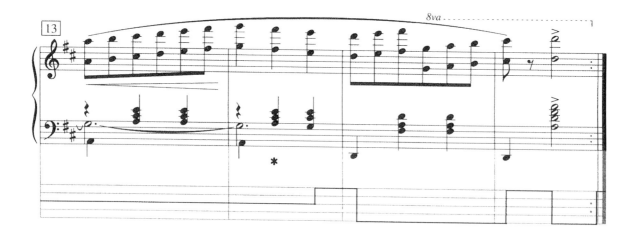

Frédéric Chopin, *Nocturne in G Minor*, op. 37, no. 1

In these excerpts, you can hear how different depths of pedal can support the proper dynamic level. This is also a good example of how shallow pedal allows for faster pedal changes. The pedal marks in the score are Chopin's and obviously must be considered when you choose your pedaling.

(a)

(b)

Robert Schumann, *Davidsbündler*, op. 6, no. 7

With rolled chords, it is important to play the bottom note exactly on the beat as you release the pedal, and to finger-pedal as much as possible until the pedal catches the bottom note of the new chord.

Go back to Lesson 2 and play the exercises and musical examples with various depths of pedal. Find examples in other repertoire where you can incorporate these techniques.

LESSON 4—SIMULTANEOUS PEDAL

Simultaneous pedaling deals with a different timing of application than syncopated pedaling, and is used most often to enhance the dynamic and tonal quality of a single note or chord or a passagework unit such as an arpeggio or a scale. Simultaneous pedal is sometimes also referred to as rhythmic or direct pedal.

Technique

In this technique, the foot depresses the damper pedal at the same time as the keys are played. The pedal may be released precisely with the release of the keys or it may be prolonged beyond. You can use any depth of pedal with this technique, depending upon the speed necessary for changes, the dynamics, and the specific effect desired.

Exercises

Exercise 1 – chords

Depress and release the pedal simultaneously with each chord, and hold for the full length of the note. Experiment with different depths and dynamics.

Exercise 2 – arpeggios

Use the same technique as in *Exercise 1*.

Exercise 3 – expressive slurs

Two-note slurs can be performed expressively by playing the second note more quietly. Sometimes two-note slurs are articulated by creating a space between the second note of one slur and the first note of the next slur. Create the space by making the second note shorter than written. When a slur is followed by a rest, always articulate the slur in this way. These are known as *articulated slurs*. Therefore, in this exercise, be sure to release both the finger and the pedal slightly before the third beat.

Exercise 4 – scales and glissandos

In this exercise, try to add a slight "sheen" to the sound with minimal pedal. Experiment with various dynamics and depths.

Music examples using simultaneous pedals

Robert Schumann, *An Important Event*, op. 15, no. 6

The simultaneous application of the pedal enhances the quality of sound. The length of the accented chords can be controlled by the release of the pedal, allowing time to prepare the hands for the next chord more comfortably.

Alexina Louie, *Shooting Stars*

This excerpt shows how the pedal can hold the full sonority of an arpeggio, creating a unit of sound by holding the bass notes as the left hand crosses over. Because the pedal changes must be quick, the player must be careful to control pedal speed and depth so as to avoid any thumping noise of the mechanism. Different depths of pedal can enhance the different dynamic levels.

Dale Reubart, *March of the Buffoons*

Here the *glissando* is heard as one sonic unit. Applying the pedal simultaneously with the first note of each *glissando* helps to emphasize the accents.

Béla Bartók, *Play*

Simultaneous pedal can help the right hand with the expressive sighing gesture in mm. 1, 2, and 4. Be sure to release the pedal and hands together so that the last note of the slur is shorter than a quarter note, as the *staccato* in the left hand indicates. In mm. 9–12, pedaling the slur in the left hand as indicated will enhance the syncopation and prevent an unwanted accent in mm. 10 and 12.

(a)

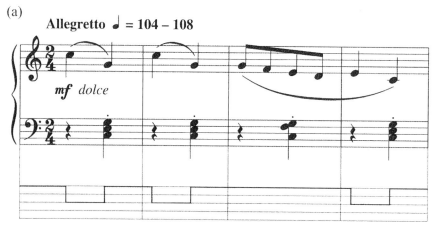

(b)

Simultaneous pedal provides sonority and accentuation in the following two examples.

Ludwig van Beethoven, *Sonata in C Major*, op. 53, third movement

Robert Schumann, *Papillons*, **op. 2, no. 3**

Frédéric Chopin, *Scherzo in B Minor*, **op. 20**
An abrupt simultaneous release of the pedal serves to accent the silence that follows it, creating a dramatic change in mood.

Franz Joseph Haydn, *Sonata in E flat Major*, **Hob. XVI:52, second movement**
The simultaneous pedals in mm. 1 and 2 help achieve the subtle articulation needed for the quarter notes. In mm. 3 and 4, these pedals help with the change in texture caused by the rests and enhance the effect of the sighing figures of the two-note slurs.

LESSON 5—GRADUAL APPLICATION OF DAMPER PEDAL

Although the piano is incapable of making a *crescendo* on one note or chord, a pianist can simulate a *crescendo*, or at least counteract the decay. To accomplish this, depress the pedal gradually—much as you would the swell pedal on an organ—so that the sympathetic vibration of all the strings is slowly added to the sound. This technique can also enhance a *crescendo* in a passage or phrase.

In music where you wish to pedal on the downbeat of every measure, a slow application of the pedal can help to make a more linear and lyric phrase, rather than emphasizing the downbeats.

Technique

In addition to applying the pedal slowly to create the impression of a *crescendo* on a single note or chord, you need to manipulate the dynamic level of the succeeding notes carefully in order to continue the effect. A slight forward movement of the body as you apply the pedal also enhances the effect. This movement not only creates a visual illusion of a *crescendo* for the audience, but also creates a physical feeling in the pianist which affects the timing and dynamic level of the following chord or note, in turn creating the illusion of growth in the tone.

Exercise

In the first four measures, try to create a *crescendo* on each whole note. In the last four measures, make a long *crescendo* for the whole phrase. Note the different levels of pedal that aid in making the long, gradual *crescendo*. At the *subito piano*, be sure to delay the attack of the note by a split second to allow the *forte* sound to clear.

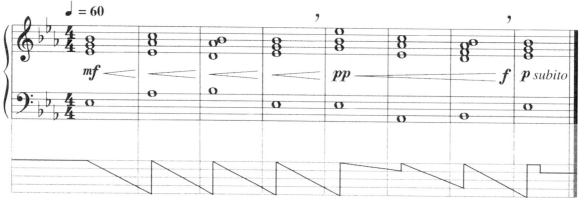

Music examples using gradual application of damper pedal

Ruth Henderson, *Lullaby in Black and White*

The subtle *crescendos* in the opening measures of this piece last for only two notes—one in the left hand and one in the right. By applying the pedal gradually, you can enhance these dynamic shapes and feel the growing tension in the melody as you lower your foot.

Vladimir Rebikov, *Waltz*

The rising shape in the first two notes of this melody calls for a *crescendo*. In addition to a slow application of the pedal, you can enhance the effect of a *crescendo* with a *rubato* that slightly stretches the time between the first two beats in mm. 1, 3, and similar places. Be sure to lift the hand at the end of slurs even though the pedal will continue to sustain the sound.

Try playing this example with the pedal indicated, then try it with the usual syncopated pedal, as explained in Lesson 2.

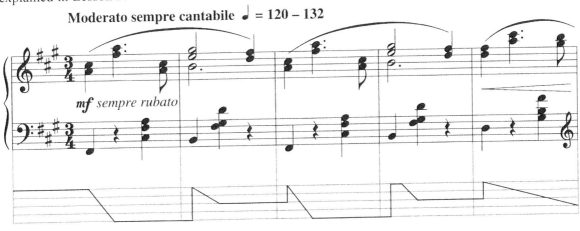

Bohdana Filtz, *A Song about Grandmother*

The indication *Andante cantabile* instructs you to perform this piece in a song-like manner. A singer would *crescendo* on the long notes to create an expressive line. The slow application of pedal on these notes can help to create the same effect.

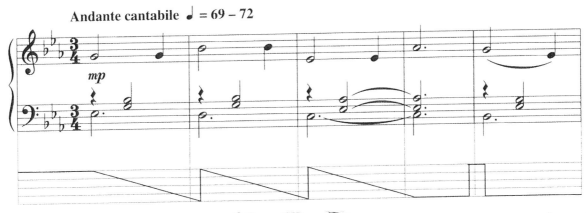

The following excerpts illustrate the same points as the preceding example. Be sure to follow the articulation given in the score, regardless of what the pedal is doing.

Pyotr Il'yich Tchaikovsky, *Morning Prayer,* **op. 39, no. 1**

Andante ♩ = 69 – 72

Frédéric Chopin, *Scherzo in C sharp Minor,* **op. 39**

(a)

Presto con fuoco ♩. = 56

(b)

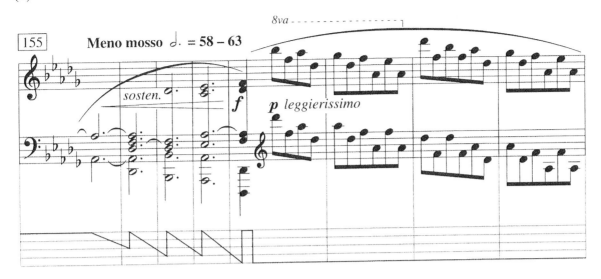

Franz Schubert, *Impromptu in G flat Major*, **op. 90, no. 3**

Robert Schumann, *Romance*, op. 28, no. 2

Franz Joseph Haydn, *Sonata in E flat Major,* **Hob. XVI:49, second movement**

In Haydn, the *fz* mark is most often intended to indicate an expressive stress, not a big dynamic accent. This example shows how a gradual pedal application can create a very subtle emphasis for the *fz*, as it will slightly enhance the sonority without an obvious dynamic accent, and will naturally cause a small agogic accent, or delay of the notes marked with *sforzandos*.

LESSON 6—GRADUAL PEDAL RELEASE

The release of a note with the pedal creates a more beautiful ending to the sound than the release of a note with the finger; with a pedal release, the damper can be returned to the strings to stop the sound more gently. Also, since raising the dampers by application of the pedal enhances the sonority, the replacement of the dampers by releasing the pedal removes some of the sonority.

- Slow, gradual pedal releases are of the greatest importance in pieces that end with a *diminuendo*.
- A gradual release of the pedal can help to create a *diminuendo* within a chord or note.
- Various combinations of finger articulation and a variety of speeds of gradual pedal releases can create a multitude of subtle lengths and colors of notes.

Technique

By gradually releasing the pedal *after* you release the finger, you can beautifully taper the ends of phrases and pieces. As a general rule, you should endeavor to use the pedal to finish the sound wherever possible. Exceptions to this rule include situations in which you want to use the simultaneous pedal technique, and places where you want a sudden cut-off of the tone in order to "accent" a following rest.

It is important to remember that the most sensitive part of the damper release is at the top, as the dampers come close to the strings. In order to taper the end of the tone, you must use the most careful control as the pedal nears the top.

An important habit to develop is to keep the hands on the surface of the keys until well after the pedaled sound has died away. Audiences tend to listen with their eyes instead of their ears at times; if the performer does not move, the listeners are drawn into concentrating on the disappearing sound and experiencing the mood this creates.

Exercises

Exercise 1 – fast application, gradual release on one chord
Listen carefully as the tone diminishes until it is inaudible at the end.

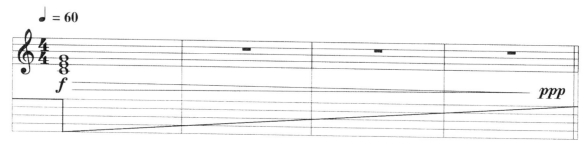

Exercise 2 – fast applications, gradual releases

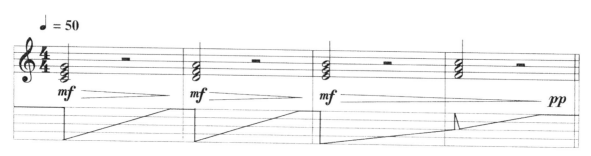

Exercise 3 – gradual pedal releases to aid in **diminuendo**

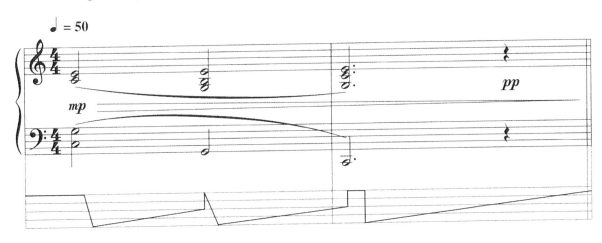

Exercise 4 – quick gradual releases

As written:

Lift the finger where indicated, followed immediately by gradual pedal release so that the tone will last the full duration of the quarter note and will have a tapered ending.

As played:

Music examples using gradual pedal release

Joanne Bender, *Inuit Lullaby*

At the end of this phrase, release the keys without anyone noticing, then gradually bring the pedal up, remembering to control it as it reaches the top. Do not move a muscle until well after all the sound has faded away.

Béla Bartók, *Children's Game*

Here is a similar ending.

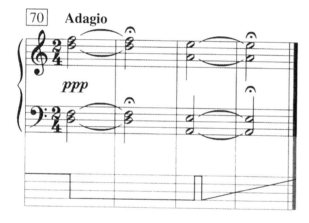

David Duke, *Barcarole*

This is another example in which gradual releases can help to create a *diminuendo*. Notice the slurs after the notes in m. 11. This notation tells the performer to pedal so that the notes continue to sound without a determinate end.

Robert Fuchs, *Timid Little Heart*, op. 47, no. 5

The gradual release of the pedal in each measure will produce a gentle ending to the left-hand phrases, which is appropriate for the character of the music.

Vladimir Rebikov, *Miniature Waltz*, op. 10, no. 10

The pedaling indicated below will support the phrasing of the music, not only dynamically but also rhythmically. You will feel the *rubato* that is called for in this piece naturally, as a result of the physical movements of slowly applying and releasing the pedal at this tempo.

Muzio Clementi, *Sonatina in F Major*, op. 36, no. 4, second movement

In this example from the Classical period, the pedal is used mostly for color, and must be applied judiciously, using a short and shallow technique. The indicated pedal employs gradual application and release to enhance the effect of *crescendo* and *diminuendo*. A gradual release works nicely in producing the appropriate effect for the *sforzandos* (mm. 7 and 8), as discussed in Lesson 5.

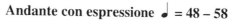

Pianos of the 19th century have a faster natural decay to their sound than do our modern instruments. As a result, it is sometimes necessary to assist the *diminuendos* of single notes or chords with a gradual release of the pedal. The following excerpts are examples of this technique.

Frédéric Chopin, *Scherzo in E Major*, op. 54

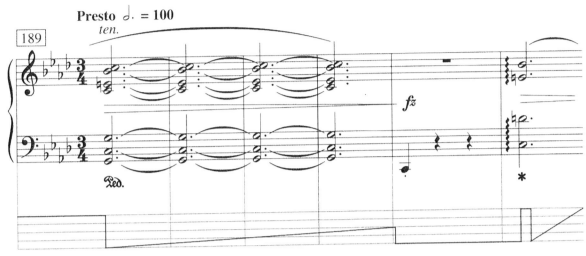

Ludwig van Beethoven, *Sonata quasi una Fantasia*, op. 27, no. 1
The following example combines simultaneous application of the pedal on the first note of each measure with slow pedal releases.

Be sure to release the fingers from the keys before releasing the pedal. The following excerpts are examples of this technique.

Claude Debussy, *Ondine* from Préludes, book II

As already demonstrated, a gradual release of the pedal provides an ethereal ending to a piece that concludes with a *diminuendo*. To taper the sound to its very end, you must exert careful control at the shallowest depth of the pedal as the dampers near the strings.

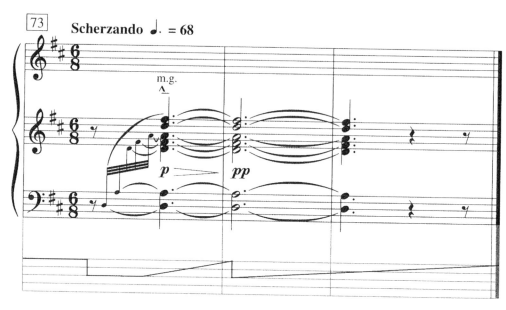

Claude Debussy, *La cathédrale engloutie* from Préludes, book I

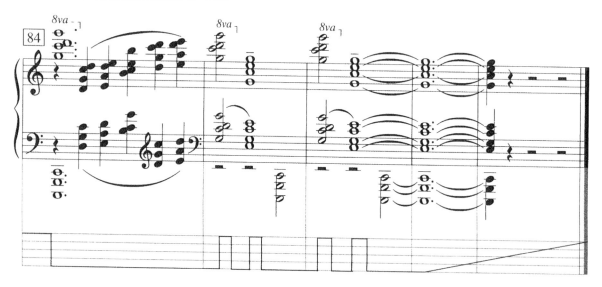

Claude Debussy, *Des pas sur la neige* from Préludes, book I

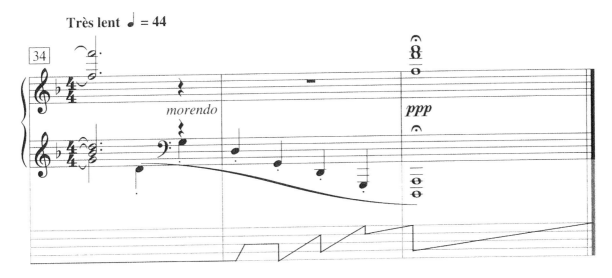

Claude Debussy, *Voiles* from Préludes, book I

The following examples show how a faster gradual release of the pedal (as learned in Exercise 4, p. 39) can provide a special ending to detached notes, which otherwise might sound too clipped on a modern piano. Carefully release the fingers slightly before you release the pedal. Experiment with timings until you get the sound and length desired. This technique also works well with *portato*.

Wolfgang Amadeus Mozart, *Eight Variations,* **K 460, Theme**

Wolfgang Amadeus Mozart, *Six Variations on an Allegretto,* **K 54**

(a)

(b)

Johann Sebastian Bach, *Fugue in D sharp Minor,* **WTC, book I**

LESSON 7—LONG PEDALS

Chopin, Liszt, and even Haydn and Beethoven often indicated long pedals throughout harmonic changes. Long pedals are also frequently implied in the music of Debussy in places where playing the music as written would require a third hand! Obviously, the only way to play such passages is by holding notes with the pedal.

As continually emphasized throughout this book, it is important to listen carefully whenever using the pedal. Listening is especially necessary when dealing with long pedals that include harmonic changes and melodic lines.

Technique—Dynamics

We must remember that composers of early periods were writing for pianos that had a more slender tone and a faster decay. Consequently, the blurred effects of long pedals did not result in a muddy sound, as can easily happen on a modern instrument.

When playing these long pedal passages on a modern instrument, much of the problem can be solved by careful voicing of the various layers of sound and by modulating the dynamics. An effective approach to accomplish this is to think of a "nest of boxes." Listen intently to the initial sonority, which is the "big box," and place each succeeding sound inside the previous sonority, just as in a set of nesting boxes. Obviously, when a *crescendo* is indicated, we must *crescendo*. At the same time, careful attention to soft voicing of the inner notes of chords will help to prevent an unpleasant sound.

Technique—Pedals

In situations where the above techniques do not completely solve the problem of muddy sound, you can clean out some overly blurred sound with careful changes of the damper pedal. Go from full pedal up to 7/8 or 3/4 depth and back down, being sure not to lose the bass note. Because the thicker low bass strings are harder to dampen than the middle and treble strings, you can get rid of some of the middle and higher sounds without losing the bass.

Exercises

Exercise 1
Depress the pedal, then play one note and listen intently to the decay until no sound remains.

Exercise 2
Depress the pedal, then play the exercise making each chord softer than the previous one. Listen intently to the decay of the sound, and match the new chord to the dynamic level of the *end* of the previous chord (rather than the level it was played).

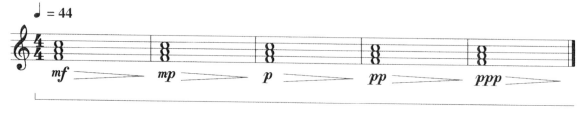

Exercise 3

Try to make a beautiful tonal effect using just dynamics and voicing. Keep listening intently to the bass note throughout, and "nest" the following notes inside that sonority.

Exercise 4

On the same passage, lift the pedal very slightly on each beat in m. 2 and at the beginning of m. 3 to clear some of the sound. Listen to the bass note, being careful not to lose it with the pedal changes. Ideally, this technique should not be necessary if voicing and modulating of dynamics is done skillfully, but certain instruments and acoustics require slight pedal lifts to thin the sound.

Music examples using long pedals

In the following examples, the composer has indicated that the pedal be held down for a long duration. Doing so should create a beautiful ethereal effect. Listen carefully for your "nest of boxes."

Boris Berlin, *The Haunted Castle*

Note that the chords are to be played detached while the pedal holds the sound. Observe the dynamics carefully.

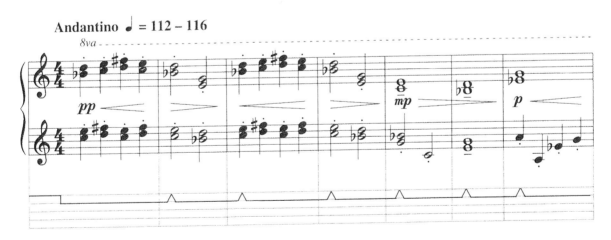

Jean Coulthard, *Star Gazing*

To create the image of the twinkling stars, pay special attention to the *staccato* articulation and the *pianissimo* dynamic.

Quite slowly

Paul Creston, *Pastoral Dance*, op. 24, no. 4

The composer has indicated that the pedal is to be held down for two measures at a time. While the left-hand harmonies are basically consonant, the melody has many non-harmonic tones. Be careful to play the non-harmonic tones more softly, and listen for a beautiful hazy sound; avoid a thick, muddy sonority.

Lyrically ♩. = 50

István Szelényi, *Faraway Regions*

The indication *con pedale* in and of itself does not mean that you should hold the pedal throughout the piece. However, Szelényi has placed specific notation across each bar line ⌢⌢ to indicate that the sound is to continue. This is indeed a pedal notation. Listen carefully to the sound created in the first measure, and place the melody in the second measure inside that sound—the "nesting boxes" technique.

Alexina Louie, *O Moon*

This piece is a wonderful example of the need for the "nest of boxes" technique. Listen carefully, and remember to fit each new sound into the existing sonorities you have already created. The *diminuendo* markings are editorial.

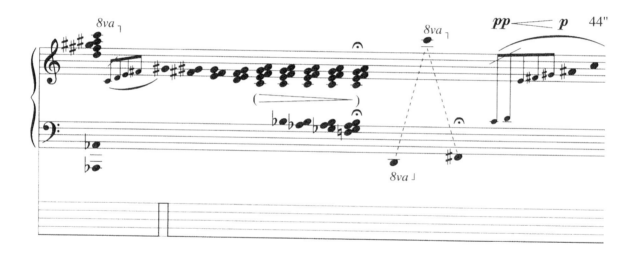

Claude Debussy, *Voiles* from Préludes, book I

Debussy often used the notation ![pedal] to indicate an indeterminate release of the pedal. These indications sometimes require that you keep the pedal down for several successive measures. When you play a number of measures in one pedal, listen carefully to the layering of sounds and the "nest of boxes" to make sure there is no unpleasant muddying of the sonority.

Claude Debussy, *Les sons et les parfums tournent dans l'air du soir* from Préludes, book I

The following examples do not include any suggested pedaling. This is a good time for you to experiment with depths and voicings before deciding whether partial releases of the pedal are necessary to achieve the desired effect. The amount of pedal needed or allowed will depend on the individual piano, the dynamics and touch used by the pianist, and the acoustics of the room. It is imperative to listen intently to the effect being produced.

Franz Joseph Haydn, *Sonata in C Major*, Hob. XVI:50, first movement

Haydn's "open pedal" for the following analogous passages in this sonata—the only pedal marks to be found in his keyboard music—indicate his wish for the coloristic effect of the blur. The measures in the bass clef should create a mysterious character, whereas the measures in the treble clef should have a music-box effect.

(a)

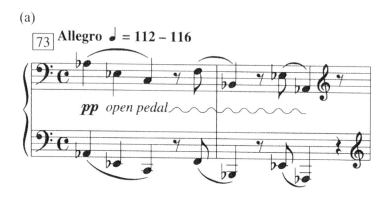

(b)

Ludwig van Beethoven, *Sonata in C Major*, op. 53, third movement

In this example, Beethoven is creating a rather "impressionist" blurred effect by changing harmonies within one pedal. It is helpful to remember that on a fortepiano of Beethoven's time, the decay was much quicker than on a modern instrument. Therefore, it usually works best to use a shallow depth of pedal along with subtle partial lifts at the harmony changes, if needed.

Ludwig van Beethoven, *Sonata in D Minor*, op. 31, no. 2, first movement

Beethoven wrote that these measures should sound like a voice from the grave. In the following two passages, listen to the decay of the sound and keep the concept of the "nest of boxes" in mind.

(a)

(b)

Frédéric Chopin, *Nocturne in D flat Major*, op. 27, no. 2

In instances such as the following, you can minimize unpleasant dissonances by playing non-harmonic melody notes more softly than notes that are part of the harmony. See the circled notes in the score.

LESSON 8—FLUTTER PEDAL

Flutter pedal is a very useful technique when you want a pedaled sound without too much blur or too thick a texture. It is useful in *portato* passages and wherever you want to give warmth to the sound without creating a pedaled effect, as well as in situations where you need a fast *diminuendo*.

Technique

Flutter-pedal technique involves a series of quick, small movements of the foot on the damper pedal. Flutter pedal can be used in connection with any pedal depth, but the range of movement must be very small.

Exercise

Music examples using flutter pedal

Ludwig van Beethoven, *Sonata in C Major***, op. 2, no. 3, first movement**

Frédéric Chopin, *Scherzo in B Minor*, op. 20

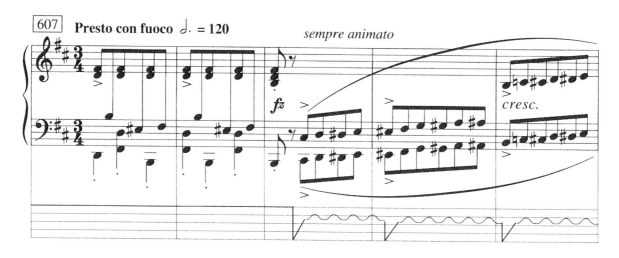

Franz Joseph Haydn, *Sonata in E flat Major*, Hob. XVI:49, second movement

A *portato* touch can be enhanced by a shallow flutter pedal. *Portato* is notated with both slurs and dots and is performed with a slight separation between notes.

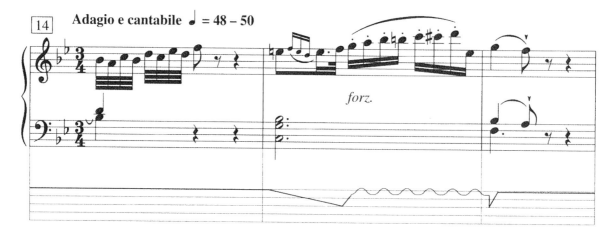

Robert Schumann, *Papillons*, op. 2, no. 1

Use a flutter pedal in the measures with eighth-note octaves. Compare the flutter pedal to the technique used on p. 24 in this example.

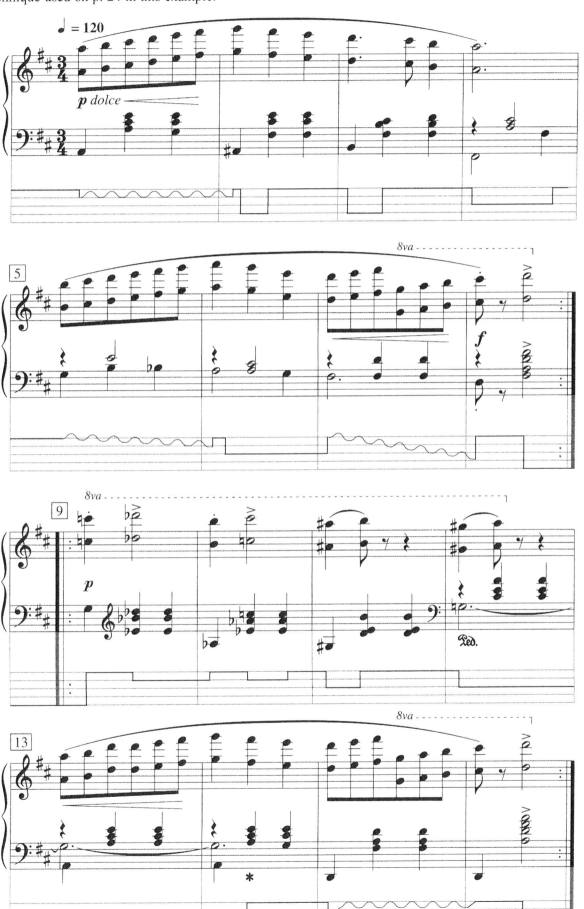

LESSON 9—PEDALING BETWEEN SLURS

In music of the Classical period, slurs are not indications of phrases but rather are akin to bowing marks for violin. In some cases, short slurs should indeed be articulated with a space between them, but in other cases they are meant to show nuances of dynamics and timing. In this latter case, although the slurs can be connected with the fingers, a much more successful and beautiful way to accomplish this effect is to lift the hand at the end of the slur and fill the hole in the sound with a quick and shallow pedal. This will create an effect much closer to the sound of a bow changing direction (more pressure at the beginning of the bow stroke, and less at the end).

Technique

Because this pedaling technique works against the meter of the music, it calls for good coordination. Depress the pedal to a shallow depth while simultaneously lifting the hand; lift the pedal as the hand plays the next note.

For the music of Mozart and Haydn, as well as much music of the Baroque period, a good approach is short, late, and shallow pedals. Here, the control at the 1/4, 1/8, and less-than-1/8 depths is absolutely essential.

Exercise

Music examples using pedaling between slurs

Wolfgang Amadeus Mozart, *Sonata in F Major*, **K 332, first movement**

Wolfgang Amadeus Mozart, *Sonata in B flat Major,* **K 333, second movement**

Ludwig van Beethoven, *Sonata in E flat Major,* **op. 31, no. 3, third movement**

LESSON 10—RETAKING THE PEDAL

The technique of retaking the pedal creates a special effect that can be used when one voice is eliminated while the rest are maintained. Such situations are found most often at the end of a piece.

Technique

Retaking the pedal involves coordination between the fingers and the foot. Follow these steps:

1. Play all the notes as written.
2. With the fingers, silently retake the notes that are to be held.
3. Release the pedal to clear the notes that are shorter than the others.
4. Reapply the pedal.
5. Release all the fingers.
6. Release the sound with the pedal.

Exercise

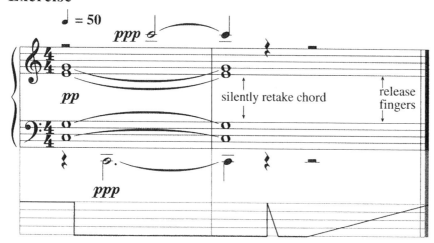

Music examples that illustrate retaking the pedal

Claude Debussy, *Danseuses de Delphes* from Préludes, book I

Claude Debussy, *Feuilles mortes* from Préludes, book II

Claude Debussy, *The Little Shepherd* from Children's Corner

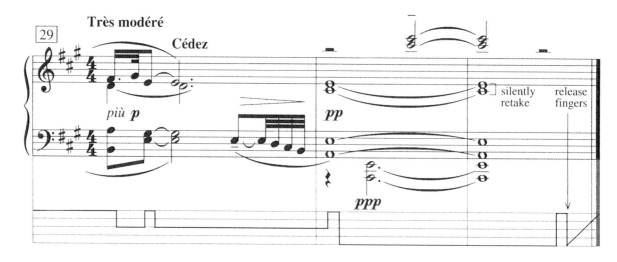

Claude Debussy, *Les sons et les parfums tournent dans l'air du soir* from Préludes, book I

In this example, be sure to hold the half notes with the left hand to the end of each measure.

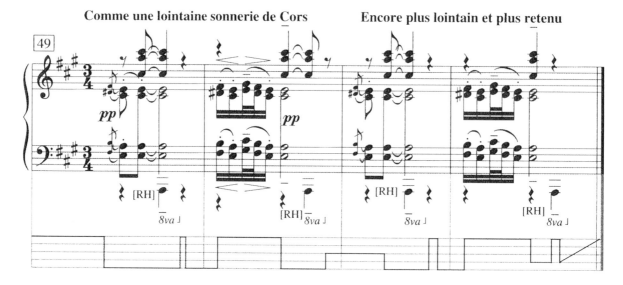

LESSON 11—*LEGATISSIMO* PEDAL

Finger *legatissimo* consists of slightly overlapping one melody note with the next in order to create an extremely *legato* sound. *Legatissimo* pedal technique serves the same purpose and can be used in places where the fingers cannot connect the notes, such as in successive chords.

Technique
This technique involves a short, gradual release and application of the pedal slightly *after* the new chord is played. The effect should be of one chord melting into the next, which calls for careful timing in order to avoid a blurry effect or dissonance.

Exercise
Experiment with timing and the speed of application and release until you achieve exactly the right effect.

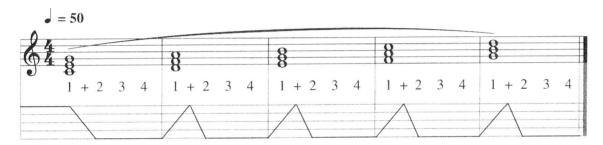

Music examples using *legatissimo* pedaling

Ludwig van Beethoven, *Sonata in F Minor*, op. 57, second movement

In this example, change the pedal on every beat, using the overlapping technique of *legatissimo* pedaling.

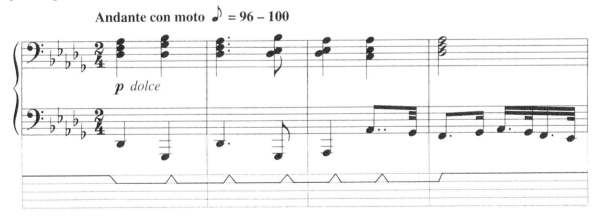

Johannes Brahms, *Intermezzo*, op. 116, no. 6

Pedal, using the overlapping technique on every beat, just as in the previous example.

Experiment with the *legatissimo* pedal technique in the exercises and musical examples in Lesson 5—Gradual Application of Damper Pedal.

THE SOFT PEDAL

History of the soft-pedal mechanism

A mechanism to soften and change the color of the sound, introduced by Bartolomeo Cristofori in 1726, soon became standard on fortepianos of the 18th century. It functioned by shifting the hammers and keyboard to the right so that only one string instead of two or three was struck. Thus, it was referred to as the *Verschiebung* (shifting) or *una corda* (one string) mechanism. Initially, the mechanism was operated by a knee lever. By 1800, the knee lever was replaced by a pedal. By the late 18th and early 19th centuries, it was possible to depress the pedal gradually in a way that would shift the mechanism from three strings (*tre corde*) to two strings (*due corde*) and then to one string (*una corda*).

The modern grand piano

The soft-pedal mechanism of a modern grand piano is much the same as that of the earlier pianos, shifting the keyboard and hammers to the right when the soft pedal is engaged. Although this pedal is still referred to as the *una corda* pedal, in octaves where there are three strings per key, the hammer hits two strings; where there are two strings per key, the hammer hits one. In the low bass where there is only one string per key, the hammer strikes the string on the left side rather than in the center.

It is important to remember that when hammers are constantly hitting strings, the hammers develop grooves of compacted felt where they contact the string. As soon as the soft pedal is engaged, the mechanism immediately moves the hammer off the grooves onto softer felt, even while striking three strings. This produces a different color of sound. When the mechanism moves all the way to its ultimate position, the hammer strikes two strings, but is back again on the impacted felt. Therefore, like the damper pedal, you can treat the soft pedal as a rheostat rather than an on-and-off light switch, creating different colors of sound in the various depths.

Upright pianos

The soft-pedal mechanism on an upright piano works differently from that of a grand piano. Instead of shifting the playing mechanism, the depressed pedal moves the hammers closer to the strings. This shorter distance results in less acceleration of the hammer, thereby reducing the force with which it hits the string and consequently the volume of the note. Because of the mechanism, the palette of colors resulting from the use of the soft pedal on an upright is less sensitive and varied than that on a grand piano.

Care of the mechanism

Pianists should be aware that the sound of the soft pedal varies greatly from one piano to another, depending on the age, voicing, and shaping of the hammers. A piano technician should shape and voice the hammers periodically to give the best and widest range of colors to the instrument. The technician should also make sure that the soft pedal engages with the slightest pressure of the foot, and that the mechanism moves the full allowable range without striking strings for two pitches.

Uses of the soft pedal

Although piano method books of the 18th and 19th centuries advocated the use of the soft pedal, it was rarely indicated in scores. However, some soft-pedal markings did begin to appear as early as Beethoven's time. Because the soft pedal is a fundamental component of the sonic possibilities of the piano, it should be used whenever the pianist finds its unique sound desirable. Keep in mind that while the soft pedal does indeed help soften the dynamics, its main purpose is to *change the color* of the sound, just as a mute does on a violin or trumpet. The soft pedal can be used at any dynamic level, not only *piano* or *pianissimo*. For example, in *Serenade of the Doll*, Debussy writes, "*Il faudra mettre la pédale sourde pendant toute la durée de ce morceau, même aux endroits marqués d'un f*" (use the soft pedal throughout the piece, even where marked *forte*).

Of course, pianists should be able to produce a soft sound using only finger technique. Therefore, you should not automatically apply the soft pedal every time the music calls for a soft dynamic, but instead reserve it for special colors and effects. Conversely, pianists should not revel in the excellence of their dynamic control to the extent that they find it a virtue never to use the soft pedal. This would deprive their interpretations of a most beautiful resource!

There are times when you encounter a piano that is too brilliant for the hall or for accompanying a voice or other instrument, or one that is too loud in the bass or too bright in the treble. The soft pedal can be employed to compensate for these problems. Similarly, you can use the soft pedal to adjust the balance between instruments in two-piano playing.

To summarize, the soft pedal may be used:
* to create a new color;
* to aid in contrast for a *subito pp*;
* to aid a *diminuendo* (add the soft pedal gradually);
* to help create a beautiful resolution (add the soft pedal on the final note or chord);
* to create special effects (use it while playing *mezzo forte, forte*, etc.);
* to compensate for a too-bright timbre or register of a particular instrument.

Notation
The common notation for the soft pedal is *u.c.* or *una corda*; the release is indicated by *t.c.* or *tre corde* (see Appendix A). While we will refer to this mechanism as the soft pedal, we will notate its use by *u.c.* (*una corda*) and its complete release by *t.c.* (*tre corde*) in the exercises and music examples in this unit.

Exercises

Exercise 1
Practice depressing the soft pedal all the way down, then 1/2 the way down, as you did in the exercises with the damper pedal. Two levels will probably be all that you will be able to do on most pianos.

Exercise 2
Play at tempo ♩ = 60, following the specific instructions. Strive to play at the same dynamic level throughout. Listen for the differences in the quantity and quality of sound.

Play with no soft pedal.

Play with soft pedal depressed 1/2 the way down.

Play with soft pedal depressed all the way.

Play the exercise while *gradually depressing* the soft pedal. Try to keep the fingers playing the same throughout, regardless of how the soft pedal affects the volume.

Exercise 3

Depress the damper pedal all the way. Do not use the soft pedal. Listen carefully to the decay of each sound and try to match each new tone with the dynamic level of the end of the previous tone.

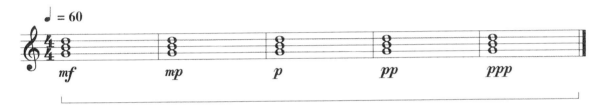

Exercise 4

Depress the damper pedal all the way, but this time gradually apply the soft pedal. Note how much easier it is to produce a *diminuendo*; notice also the beautiful colors you can create.

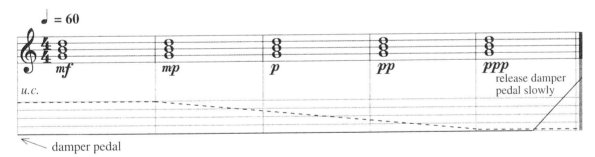

Exercise 5

Play the following cadence without the soft pedal. Listen carefully to the final decay of the first chord, and then play the second chord softer than that sound. Play the cadence again, this time with the soft pedal. Be sure that the soft pedal is depressed *before* you play the final chord.

Playing music examples using soft pedal

After mastering the above exercises for the soft pedal and heightening your awareness of the difference in sonorities, go back to the musical examples in Unit One, especially in Lessons 2, 6, 7, and 10. Experiment with adding soft pedal to create different colors, to achieve a softer dynamic, or to help with *diminuendos*.

THE SOSTENUTO PEDAL

History of the *sostenuto* pedal

Although the middle-pedal mechanism, known as the *sostenuto* or sustaining pedal, was invented by a French firm in 1844, it was not patented until 1874 by Steinway & Sons, New York. You will encounter relatively few markings for its use, even in 20th-century music. However, several late 20th-century composers indicate its use for special effects.

The *sostenuto*-pedal mechanism is found on most grand pianos. Its purpose is to sustain some notes while other notes are detached. To engage the mechanism, you must hold down the notes you wish to sustain when you depress the pedal. The mechanism then holds those dampers up, while you play *detaché* on other notes.

Many upright pianos have a middle pedal, but it is often either a dummy pedal or a type of mute to be used only for quiet practicing. When the middle pedal on an upright is indeed a sustaining mechanism, it most often functions only for the lower half of the keyboard.

Here are some important points to note:

- Do not engage the damper pedal while depressing the *sostenuto* pedal. Doing so would hold up all the dampers.
- Keep the *sostenuto* pedal fully depressed for the entire time you wish the sounds to be prolonged.
- The *sostenuto* pedal feels different and operates differently on every piano. Unfortunately, this mechanism is seldom properly regulated, even in concert hall instruments. It is wise not to depend on it unless you know the instrument on which you will be performing.

Uses of the *sostenuto* pedal

It is important to know when *not* to use the *sostenuto* pedal from a stylistic standpoint.

1. Avoid using it in the music of Debussy. While he was aware of the mechanism, he was simply not interested in it, and his piano did not have a *sostenuto* pedal. The intended blurred effect of long pedal points in Debussy's music must be accomplished by skillful use of the damper pedal, voicing of dynamic levels, and finger articulation (see Unit One, Lesson 7).

2. Avoid its use unless it is specifically indicated—particularly in music of the 19th century. This is not only because of the unreliability of the mechanism and the need for split-second timing, but also because the music was not written with these special effects in mind.

3. Obviously, the *sostenuto* pedal should be used whenever the composer so indicates. If you are very skillful with its use, the *sostenuto* pedal can be used in combination with the damper pedal in certain instances, such as:
   - holding bass pedal points;
   - playing with contrasting touches within a pedal point;
   - catching notes within chords;
   - holding implied pedal points;
   - creating special acoustic effects by silently depressing harmonic notes and catching them in the *sostenuto* pedal before playing.

For a complete discussion of these techniques, see *The Pianist's Guide to Pedaling* by Joseph Banowetz.[1]

Notation

This pedal is most often indicated by *sost. ped.* or *S.P.* ⌐‾‾‾‾‾‾‾‾‾‾⌐ ; the line indicates the duration it is to be held. However, there are instances where the release of the pedal is not indicated, which can lead to some confusion.

Exercise

Be sure to hold the bass note down until the sostenuto pedal is engaged.

Music examples using the *sostenuto* pedal

Steven Gellman, *Introspection*

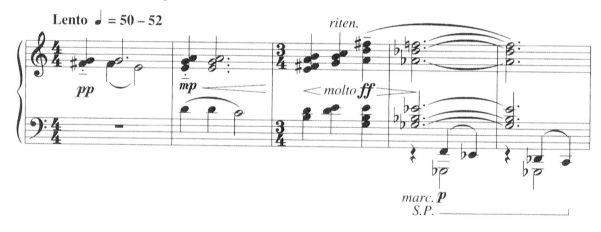

[1] Joseph Banowetz, *The Pianist's Guide to Pedaling*. Bloomington: Indiana University Press, 1985.

Samuel Barber, *Sonata for Piano*

Aaron Copland, *Piano Variations*

Più largamente ancora ♩ = 58

74

STYLISTIC PRINCIPLES OF PEDALING

While the use of the pedals is largely a matter of personal taste, we should be familiar with stylistic contemporary practices in pedaling that can and should influence our choices. Particularly in music written for harpsichord and early fortepianos, we must essentially make a "translation" from the original instrument to the modern piano, using more or less pedal as needed to produce sounds that are closest to an authentic sound. It is extremely important to use good Urtext scores when dealing with the pedaling of these composers, rather than relying on editions in which there is no clear differentiation between the composer's original notation and the editor's suggestions or where the markings may not be accurately placed.

The following is a brief guide to some of the pedaling techniques associated with selected composers from various style periods.

PEDALING BAROQUE MUSIC

J.S. Bach
Baroque keyboard instruments
Bach's keyboard music was written for harpsichord, clavichord, or organ, none of which has the pedal mechanisms of the piano. However, when "translating" these works to the piano, it is not only justified but necessary to use the resources of the modern instrument, which include both dynamic capabilities and pedals.

The damper pedal
Pianists should be careful to use the damper pedal in such a way that the sonority does not become too thick. Melodic or polyphonic textures should not be compromised; in other words, no two consecutive notes in a melodic line should be played in the same pedal.

The damper pedal may be used:
- to enhance the beauty of individual notes or chords—use either syncopated- or simultaneous-pedal techniques;
- to enhance *legato* and *cantabile*—use short, shallow, and late pedals;
- for accentuation—use simultaneous pedal technique;
- wherever finger-pedaling is possible or desirable—such as in arpeggios—use simultaneous- or flutter-pedal technique;
- to counteract decay on a long melody note or a single chord—use slow application;
- to hold a bass note momentarily when a leap occurs immediately afterward.

Una corda pedal
In addition to helping produce a soft dynamic, the use of the *una corda* pedal is appropriate in music where a change of color is needed to create contrast, as in terraced dynamics, and to represent changes of registration on the harpsichord or organ.

Sostenuto pedal
The *sostenuto* pedal can be used to help sustain long pedal points sometimes found in works written for harpsichord and in transcriptions of works written for organ and other instruments.

PEDALING CLASSICAL MUSIC

Mozart and *Haydn*
Late 18th-century fortepiano

Early Viennese fortepianos have a silvery and clear sound, with a distinct difference in color between the low, middle, and high registers. The tone is slender. While these instruments can play much softer than the modern piano, they cannot play as loudly. Also, because the sound decays much faster than on a modern piano, careful listening is needed to match tones and shape phrases.

Mozart never indicated the use of the damper mechanism, although we know from his letters and other sources that he used the device. Haydn indicated the use of the dampers in only one work (see p. 54), but scholars assume he also used the damper mechanism in the prevailing stylistic manner, as explained below.

Damper mechanism

The Viennese fortepianos of this period had damper mechanisms operated either with hand stops or, more commonly, with knee levers. The knee levers were sometimes divided so that either the bass or treble dampers could be raised independently.

Here are some guidelines for translating to the modern piano.
- When playing music of this period, endeavor to create a slender tone and clarity of sound by using *short*, *shallow*, and *late* pedal applications.
- Bass notes on the fortepiano are clear, never muddy (as they can be on a modern instrument). Therefore, generally use little or no pedal when dealing with thick bass textures in music of this period.
- Because the tone of a modern piano is very dry compared to the sound of a fortepiano, there is a tendency to use more pedal than performers on the fortepiano would. However, great discretion and subtlety is required.

Stylistic use of the damper pedal
1. Change when the harmonies change.
2. Let the pedal "breathe" with the phrasing.
3. Do not allow the pedal to undo articulated slurs (see p. 28) and other articulation markings.
   Note: The technique discussed in Lesson 9 should not negate slurs if they are executed properly.
4. Do not pedal through rests, as they are to be observed literally.
5. Pedal may be used to enhance tonal effects, such as louder dynamics or notes requiring emphasis.

Una corda and moderator mechanisms

In addition to the *una corda* mechanism used to create softer sounds and variations of color, fortepianos often have a "moderator." When engaged by a knee lever or hand stop, the moderator places a strip of felt between the strings and hammers, creating an incredibly soft and ethereal effect. The soft pedal can be used where a very soft dynamic and special color is desired.

Beethoven
Mechanisms

The foot pedal was invented in 1783, but for his early works, Beethoven was most likely still using a piano with knee levers. His later Broadwood piano had pedals on the legs of the piano: the damper on the right and the soft pedal on the left. An interesting feature was a split damper pedal. Pressing the right part of the pedal raised the treble dampers, the left part raised the bass dampers, and the whole pedal raised the dampers for the entire keyboard.

The soft pedal (*Verschiebung*, or shifting) could move the mechanism from three strings (*tre corde* or *tutte le corde*) to two strings (*due corde*) to one (*una corda*). Beethoven wrote these specific pedal instructions in many of his works.

Notation

Beethoven was the one of the first composers to indicate pedal. In his early published works, he indicated the use of the damper pedal by writing *senza sordino* (without dampers, meaning with the damper pedal on) or *con sordino* (with the dampers, meaning without the pedal). After about 1802, he began to use the marking *Ped.* for application of the pedal, and O for its release. Modern Urtext editions use ✳ for the release sign.

Uses

Beethoven's students Czerny and Hummel said he used a lot of pedal. One has to wonder how much Beethoven's deafness affected his use of the pedal in his own playing. However, in his scores, we find nearly eight hundred indications for the use of the pedals, almost all of which were for the damper mechanism. His music calls for the use of pedal for a variety of reasons:

* to create ethereal effects with long pedals;
* to promote *legato;*
* to create fullness of sound;
* to connect movements;
* to aid in even graduations of *crescendos* and *diminuendos*. An interesting example is in the third movement of the *Sonata in A flat Major*, op. 110, where he indicates *una corda* and damper pedal for this purpose. Note the markings in the excerpt that follows.

Ludwig van Beethoven, *Sonata in A flat Major*, op. 110, third movement

It is clear that in his innovative use of pedals, Beethoven's "sound ideal" brings him closer to the Romantic than to the Classical composers.

PEDALING ROMANTIC MUSIC

In Romantic piano music, the pedaled sound became the norm around 1820, with the piano expected to vibrate almost constantly, like the *vibrato* on stringed instruments. A dry sound is the exception, almost a special effect. The emphasis on the use of the pedals was a result of a new concern with sonority and instrumental color during the Romantic period.

Although their music depended on an extensive use of the pedal, most composers were still sparing in their indications of when it should be used. Even when pedal is indicated, it may not seem to work on a modern instrument. Charles Rosen makes an important point in his book *The Romantic Generation*:

> The first question, in time as well as importance, is: Why did the composer indicate the pedal? Or more precisely: What is the function of the pedal in a given passage? The pedal has two different basic functions (as well as some subsidiary ones): it sustains struck notes, and it allows those which are not struck to vibrate in sympathy. Until this distinction is clear, no sensible observation can be made about the notations for pedalling on late eighteenth- and early nineteenth-century instruments.[1]

---

[1] Charles Rosen, *The Romantic Generation.* Cambridge: Harvard University Press, 1995, p. 140.

Even when the pedal is not indicated, it is probably safe to assume that it is to be used. Romantic composers would have assumed that:

- the pedal would be changed when the harmony changed;
- phrasing is shaped by the pedal (changes of pedal are crucial for rhythm and melodic line, as well as for harmony);
- one usually would not pedal through rests.

Schubert

Schubert indicated pedal very rarely, even though the Graf fortepiano that was his favorite had at least three pedals: damper, soft, and moderator.

One of Schubert's pedal notations is found in the slow movement of his *Sonata in B flat Major*, D 960. The staccato marks on the bass notes mean they are to be played lightly, with the sound to be held by the pedal. The sonority thus created anticipated the style of playing for years to come.

Franz Schubert, *Sonata in B flat Major*, D 960, second movement

An example of a similar notation of the bass accompaniment where the pedal is not indicated occurs in Schubert's *Fantasia in C Major,* D 605a.

Franz Schubert, *Fantasia in C Major* ("Grazer Fantasie"), D 605a

Beethoven also used this type of notation in the accompaniment. It is a modern sonority found in the works of Chopin and many others. It is clear that in these instances, the pedal, whether indicated or not, should be used to sustain the bass.

Schubert did not specify the use of the soft pedal, but it should be used. It is likely that his ***ppp*** markings would have called for use of the moderator pedal, which creates the softest and most ethereal sound. The *una corda* pedal is certainly appropriate in such sections, as well as in those marked *pp*.

Mendelssohn

Mendelssohn marked some of his works quite abundantly, but in others he left no markings at all, except possibly *sempre con (col) pedale* at the beginning. As with other composers who used similar markings, his use of this term indicated that pedaling should be done according to personal taste and was assumed to be a part of the overall sound.

Chopin

Although pedal is essential for playing Chopin properly, there are few reliable reports on his own pedaling. Some said he used it too much, and some said he used it with reserve. Probably the most specific was Antoine-François Marmontel, a brilliant pianist and teacher who often heard Chopin play. Marmontel wrote that Chopin used the pedals in a completely individual way, with a marvelous sensitivity:

> Sometimes he coupled the pedals to obtain a soft, veiled sonority, but often, he used them separately for brilliant passages, sustained harmonies, low bass notes, and forceful, dazzling chords. He used the soft pedal alone for those light murmurings that seem to surround the arabesques that adorn the melody in a transparent vapor and *envelop* it as delicate lace. The timbre produced by the pedals of Pleyel's pianos has a perfect sonority.[2]

According to Arthur Hedley, "It was often observed that [Chopin's] foot seemed literally to vibrate as he rapidly pedaled certain passages." [3]

Of all composers, Chopin wrote the most extensive and careful pedaling indications; his manuscripts show many erasures and crossings-out. This poses an important question: What should we do when no pedal is indicated?

In the 20th century, pianists commonly stated that where Chopin indicated no pedal the pedaling required is very simple, and is therefore self-evident; or on the contrary, it is so subtle as to be too complicated, if not impossible to indicate. However, if you examine Chopin's pedal markings in manuscripts and Urtext editions, it is apparent that Chopin was clearly aware of the difference in texture and tone between the pedaled and unpedaled sounds. The following excerpts, in which similar passages are consistently marked with and without pedal, is a case in point.

Frédéric Chopin, *Mazurka in A flat Major*, op. 59, no. 2

(a)

(b)

---

[2] Antoine François Marmontel, *Histoire du piano et de ses origines.* Paris: Heugel, 1885, pp. 254, 256-257. Quoted in Sandra P. Rosenblum, "Some Enigmas of Chopin's Pedal Indications," *Journal of Musicological Research*, 16.1 (1996), 42.

[3] Arthur Hedley, *Chopin*, 3rd ed. Rev. Maurice Brown. London: Dent, 1974, p. 123.

Another issue in Chopin's music is where to release the pedal. We cannot assume that 𝄢 ＊ 𝄢 ＊ always indicates overlapping pedal or syncopated pedaling, as this technique had not yet become standard. Sometimes it works very well to lift at the end of the measure. In the above example, which is visually correct in its reproduction of the placement of pedal marks in the manuscript, we can see that Chopin varies the placement of the release sign—sometimes before, sometimes on, and occasionally after the third beat of the measure.

Although Chopin did not indicate the *una corda* pedal, one of his students wrote that, "Chopin ... used the pedal, particularly the soft pedal—without, however, indicating this to his pupils, in order not to overstep or exaggerate its resources." Another student wrote that Chopin advised, "Learn to make a *diminuendo* without the help of the [*una corda*] pedal; you can add it later."[4]

In making decisions about the use of the pedals in Chopin's music, we must conclude that the proper approach is to use good Urtext editions, study the notation carefully, consider what most likely was the intended effect, and then take into account the translation from the early 19th-century Pleyel piano to the modern piano. As Sandra Rosenblum says in the concluding sentence of her article on Chopin's pedaling: "We may not observe every notated sign for pedaling (Chopin often changed his), but our knowledge and general use of this historical information can inspire fresh and sensitive performances with a new point of view."[5]

Schumann

Robert Schumann often just wrote *Col pedale* or a similar instruction at the beginning of a piece, leaving the decisions throughout to the performer. In his first and second editions (1836 and 1840), Schumann wrote the following footnote: "The composer uses the pedal in nearly every measure, always as the changes of harmony demand. Exceptions, where he wishes that it not be used are marked ⊕ with the next *"Pedale"* marking, its constant use begins again."[6] Around this same time, Schumann began to write successive pedal signs (*Ped.*) without corresponding release signs, a practice which is common in Liszt's music as well. Schumann makes a telling comment in a letter of 21 September 1837 to A. Henselt: "At the beginnings of my compositions I, too, put nothing but 'Pedal,' so it must sometimes produce quite new effects when the accent has to fall on the second beat."[7]

---

[4] Quotations from Rosenblum, "Some Enigmas of Chopin's Pedal Indications," *Journal of Musicological Research*, 16.1 (1996), 58.

[5] Ibid.

[6] Robert Schumann, *Grande Sonate pour le Pianoforte composé et dediée à Mademoiselle Clara Wieck Pianiste de S.M. l'Empereur d'Autriche*, op. 11, 2nd ed. Leipzig: Friedrich Kistner, 1840, quoted in Joseph Banowetz, *The Pianist's Guide to Pedaling*. Bloomington: Indiana University Press, 1985, p. 199.

[7] Ibid.

Schumann was also inventive with his use of the damper pedal, introducing some unusual pedal effects, such as in the finale of *Papillons*, where he calls for a twenty-seven-measure pedal on D in the bass, combined with the "Grossvater Tanz" tune in the tenor and the melody of No. 1 in the soprano. He also indicated a twelve-measure pedal in the closing of "Florestan" in *Carnaval*. For a special effect, he also placed signs for releasing the pedal that go against changes of harmony.

Schumann indicated the use of the soft pedal with the word "Verschiebung." Clara Schumann's edition of her husband's music, in which she provides additional pedaling marks, may give us some insight into Robert Schumann's general outlook on pedaling.

Liszt

There is evidence that Liszt used syncopated pedal as early as 1824, although that technique was not generally used until 1860. Like Schumann, he often wrote successive pedal marks without indicating when to release the pedal. In some pieces, Liszt wrote *harmonioso*, a direction to use the damper pedal to blend harmonies. The texture of his music calls for liberal use of the damper pedal even when not notated. When he wanted no pedal, he wrote *senza pedale*.

Liszt used the pedals to help color extra-musical pictorial images. He usually indicated the soft pedal by writing *una corda* and *les deux Pédales* when he wanted damper and soft pedals used together. The use of soft pedal was not always combined with soft dynamics.

Brahms

Brahms wrote very few pedaling indications. Except in a few places where he wanted special effects, Brahms left it up to performers to make their own pedaling decisions, assuming that they would take into account his cross-rhythms and harmonic structures.

PEDALING IMPRESSIONIST MUSIC

Debussy and *Ravel*

The pedal in the music of Debussy and Ravel is integral to the art of Impressionism with its emphasis on color, sonority and "sound for sound's sake." Although these composers rarely indicated pedal, careful attention to notation and an understanding of the aesthetic of the time can lead pianists to the appropriate use of the pedals. Debussy especially was very precise in his notation concerning the fingers and feet. The stylistic sound of Impressionism depends on a number of factors, including careful attention to the articulation—*staccatos*, slurs indicating *legato* touch, and *portato*—as well as a myriad of subtle touches that can be used from a finger technique standpoint.

Here are some guidelines for pedaling Impressionist music.
- Long bass notes, sometimes tied over several measures, are an indication to use the damper pedal. (Debussy did not intend the use of the *sostenuto* pedal.)
- Debussy often indicates the pedal with long, curved lines either at noteheads, or across bar lines ⌒. He also wrote *laissez vibrer* (allow to vibrate).
- Muddy or thick texture is to be avoided at all times. This can be accomplished by careful voicing and attention to dynamics of the different layers of the musical texture. A good analogy is to think of the music as a painting with a *foreground* (melody), *middle ground* (bass line), and *background* (all else, including inner notes of chords and octave doublings). The "nest of boxes" concept will also help to prevent muddiness, as will the use of shallow pedals and flutter-pedal technique.
- When no long pedal is called for, the pianist should pedal normally: changing the pedal when the harmonies change, not pedaling through solo melodies, and not pedaling through rests. When Debussy wished absolutely no pedal, he wrote *sec* or *très sec* (dry or very dry).

- Although Debussy only rarely indicates the use of the soft pedal (by writing *una corda*), the subdued dynamic palette of his music calls for the use of the soft pedal at the discretion of the performer to distinguish clearly between *p*, *pp*, *più pp*, and ***ppp*** dynamic levels.

There are a number of examples of the use of the damper pedal in the music of Debussy in this book, especially in Lessons 6, 7, and 10.

PEDALING CONTEMPORARY MUSIC

By the beginning of the 20th century, composers were becoming more precise in their use of notation, including that for the pedals. Today, most composers indicate the use of the damper pedal with └────∧────┘ rather than the ℘ℰ∂. ✳ marks, and some contemporary composers create their own unique notations, which are self-explanatory. The word *sec* has become an accepted indication for an unpedaled sound. Special effects possible with the *sostenuto* pedal continue to be explored. The *una corda* pedal is often indicated, but performers will undoubtedly continue to make their personal decisions as to its use.

The music of the 20th century and beyond is not characterized by any one style. Consequently, we cannot make generalizations about use and notation of pedaling, as is possible to at least some degree for earlier eras. However, the pedaling techniques and concepts discussed throughout this book are applicable to contemporary music. In any musical performance, the decisions regarding pedal depth, applications, and releases must ultimately be based on the knowledge, insight, and taste of the performer.

For more extensive information on the stylistic use of the pedals of a number of composers discussed in this unit, see Appendix B—Select Bibliography.

The following examples combine the various techniques of the damper pedal and the soft pedal. Play each example first using just the damper pedal where indicated, and then just the soft pedal. Be sure that your fingers are always executing the indicated articulations, whether or not the damper pedal is engaged. When you have mastered the coordination between the hands and each pedal, practice with both pedals until you can play the example with ease. Remember to listen carefully to all the colors and sounds you create. Ultimately your ear will guide your pedaling.

Domenico Scarlatti, *Sonata in D Minor*, L 413, K 9

Some pianists mistakenly believe that pedal is not appropriate in Baroque music. The dry sound of the piano can be enlivened with touches of both damper and soft pedals (if used judiciously) without changing the basic non-*legato* touch to a *legato* one. The higher the register on the piano, the more damper pedal you can use without blurring the sound.

Note: All articulation and dynamic marks in this excerpt are editorial.

Muzio Clementi, *Sonatina in F Major*, op. 36, no. 4, second movement
In this excerpt, as in all music of the Classical period, the pedal technique must be subtle and refined, and should be worked out thoughtfully. Short, shallow, and late applications of the damper pedal and touches of the soft pedal can be used to color the sound and mold the phrasing without thickening the sonority or muddying the clarity.

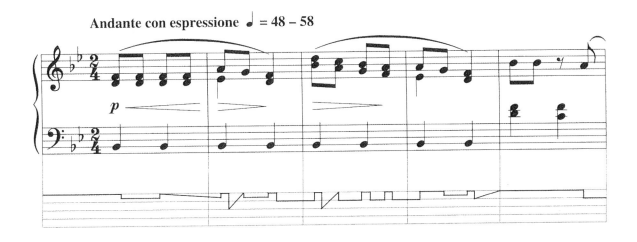

Wolfgang Amadeus Mozart, *Sonata in C Major*, K 330, second movement

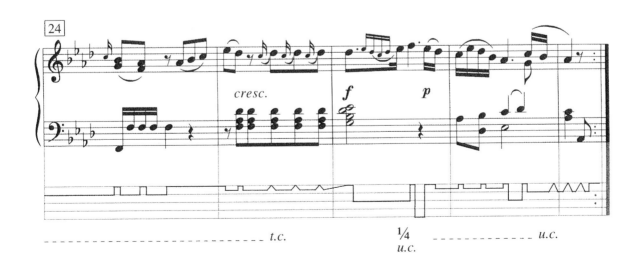

t.c.

Franz Schubert, *Impromptu in A flat Major*, op. 142, no. 2

This excerpt is a good example of the wide range of dynamics found in Schubert's music. Be sure to voice the top notes of the chords; the melody must sing, regardless of the dynamic level or whether the soft pedal is employed.

Allegretto ♩ = 96 – 112

u.c. - t.c.

Robert Schumann, *A Little Romance*, op. 68, no. 19

Be careful to observe the finger articulations accurately. Note how the pedals enhance the dynamics and accentuations.

Grigori Frid, *A Little Rain (Etude)*

The rain can be made a little "wetter" by adding 1/8 pedal or less, as indicated. Keep the *staccatos* very short. This combination of shallow pedals and short *staccatos* creates a charming sound; listeners will not realize you are pedaling.

Moderato ♩ = 100 – 108

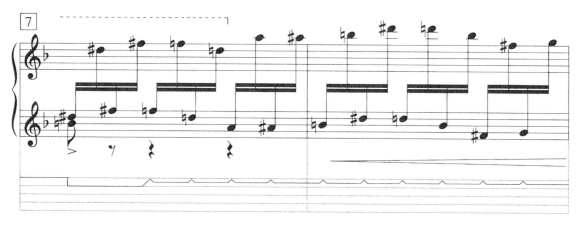

dim. poco a poco

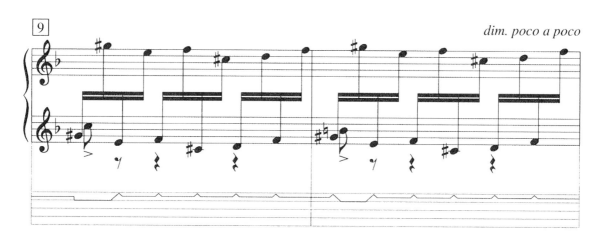

8va - - - - - - -

½ *u.c.* - - - - - - - - - - - - - -

Carl Maria von Weber, *Waltz in G Major*, op. 4, no. 2

TRIO

Fine

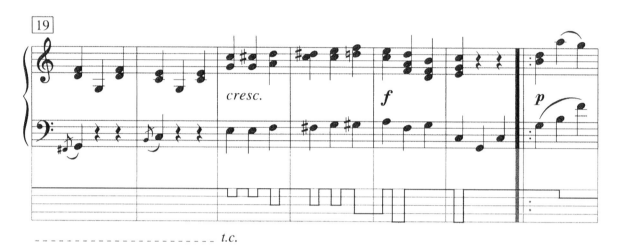

u.c. _ _ _ _ _ _ _ _ _

_ t.c.

D.C. al Fine

Dale Reubart, *Bolero*

This excerpt illustrates how the combination of finger *staccato*, damper pedal, and soft pedal can create the ethereal effect called for by the composer in his instructions to play "slowly, dreamily."

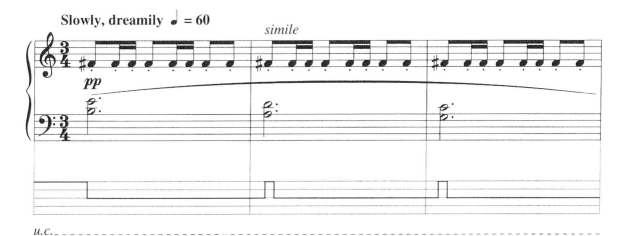

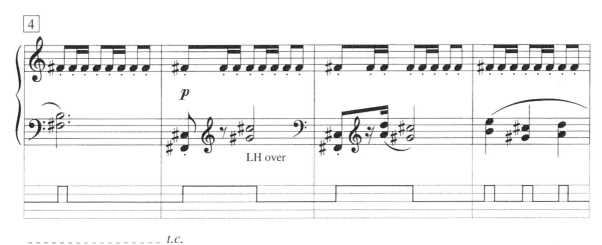

Steven Gellman, *Introspection*

The *sostenuto* pedal is indicated by the composer, so this piece requires the use of all three pedals. Coordination of both feet with both hands is tricky but essential. Be particularly careful when applying the *sostenuto* pedal; it must engage at the right time. Here are a few suggestions:

- mm. 1, 7, 20, and 24—be sure to engage the soft pedal exactly where indicated.
- mm. 3 and 4—the pedal should be released with the left-hand *staccato* while you still hold the right-hand chord, then reapplied in order to connect the chords in the right hand.
- mm. 7, 8, 23, and 24—start the rolled chords on the beat, changing the pedal in such a way so as to catch the bass notes in the new pedal.
- mm. 7 and 8—if you cannot hold the low E in the last chord in m. 7 over the bar line, silently retake the E before releasing the pedal at the beginning of m. 8, so that you hear the E momentarily sounding alone. To make a lovely ending to the *staccato* E, let go of the key, then release with the pedal as indicated. This should leave a slight space of silence before the start of the next rolled chord.

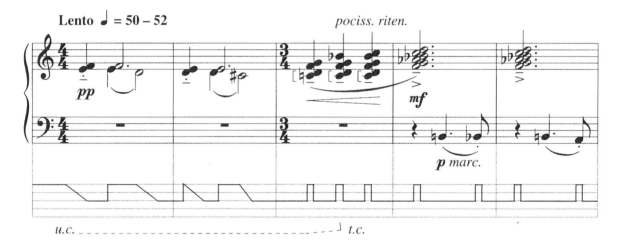

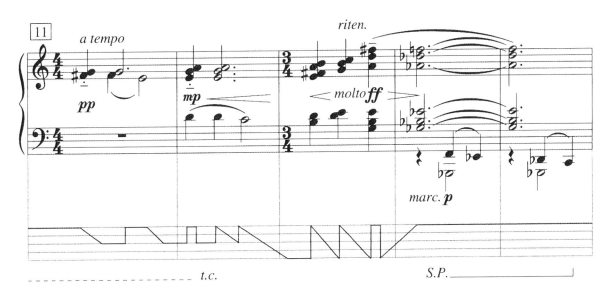

Poco più mosso ♩ = 60 – 62

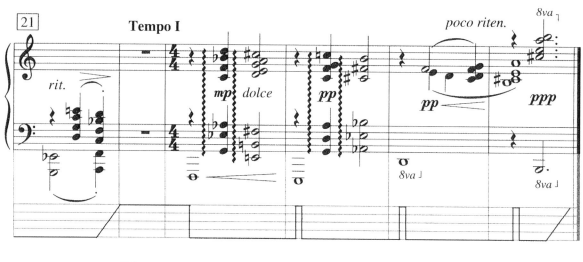

t.c.   u.c.

APPENDIX A
Terminology and Notation for the Pedals

Although individual composers occasionally devise their own notation for pedaling, the following terminology and notation are used most often.

The Right Pedal

Terminology
The following terms all indicate use of the damper pedal:

English: damper pedal, loud pedal, open pedal, sustaining pedal, amplifying pedal

French: *avec pédale, la pédale forte, pédale grande, gardez la pédale*

German: *das Aushaltpedal, das Dämpferpedal, das Dämpfungspedal, der Fortezug, das grosse Pedal, mit Pedalgebrauch*

Italian: *col pedale, con pedale, il primo pedale, pedale del forte, sempre pedale, senza sordini*

Notation
Older styles of indicating application and release of the damper pedal include:

Ped. *

Ped. O

Current notation indicates application and release with brackets:

The following indicate no pedal or release of the pedal:

con sordini (with dampers)

non ped. or *sans ped.*

ohne ped.

sec or *très sec*

secco

senza ped.

The Left Pedal

Terminology
The following terms are most often used to indicate use of the left pedal on a modern piano.
una corda

u.c.

Verschiebung

sordini

sourdine

1 corde

The following terms indicate the release of the left pedal:
tre corde

t.c.

3 c.

ohne Verschiebung

tutte le corde

Notation
There is no notation for the left pedal other than the terminology given above.

The Sostenuto *Pedal*

Terminology
sustaining pedal
prolonging pedal
sostenuto pedal

Notation
S.P. ⌐____⌐
3. Ped or *Ped. 3*
prolongement
sost. ped.

APPENDIX B
Select Bibliography

Badura-Skoda, Paul. *Interpreting Bach at the Keyboard*. Trans. Alfred Clayton. New York: Oxford University Press, 1993.

Banowetz, Joseph. *The Pianist's Guide to Pedaling*. Bloomington: Indiana University Press, 1985.

Bernstein, Seymour. "The Pedals," *Earth Music Series*, book 4. New York: Schroeder & Gunther, 1984.

————. *With Your Own Two Hands*. New York: Schirmer, 1981.

Bilson, Malcolm. "The Soft Pedal Revisited," *The Piano Quarterly* 30 (Spring 1982), 36–38.

Bowen, York. *Pedaling the Modern Pianoforte*. London: Oxford University Press, 1964.

Carreño, Teresa. *Possibilities of Tone Color by Artistic Use of Pedals*. Cincinatti: Church, 1919.

Dumesnil, Maurice. *How to Play and Teach Debussy*. New York: Schroeder & Gunther, 1932.

Eigeldinger, Jean-Jacques. *Chopin: Pianist and Teacher as Seen by His Pupils*. Trans. Naomi Shohet. Cambridge: Cambridge University Press, 1986.

Gebhard, Heinrich. *The Art of Pedaling*. New York: Franco Colombo, 1963.

Higgins, Thomas. *Chopin Interpretation: A Study of Performance Directions in Selected Autographs and Other Sources*. Ph.D. diss., University of Iowa, 1966.

Hopkins, Edwina Patricia. *The Use of Pedal in J.S. Bach's French Suites, English Suites, and Partitas: A General Guide to Pedaling in the Keyboard Music*. Ph.D. diss., Ohio State University, 1980.

Leimer, Karl, and Walter Gieseking. *Rhythmics, Dynamics, Pedal, and Other Problems of Piano Playing*, 1938. Repr. in *Piano Technique*. New York: Dover, 1972.

Mallard, Betty Parker. *Performance Instructions in the Preludes and Etudes of Claude Debussy*. Ph. D. diss., University of Texas, 1979.

Neuhaus, Heinrich. *The Art of Piano Playing*. Trans. K.A. Leibovitch. New York: Praeger, 1973.

Newman, William S. *Beethoven on Beethoven*. New York: Norton, 1988.

Riefling, Reimar. *Piano Pedaling*. Trans. Kathleen Dale. London: Oxford University Press, 1962.

Rosen, Charles. *The Romantic Generation*. Cambridge: Harvard University Press, 1995.

Rosenblum, Sandra P. "Pedaling the Piano: A Brief Survey from the Eighteenth Century to the Present." *Performance Practice Review* 6.2 (1993), 158–178.

————. *Performance Practices in Classic Piano Music*. Bloomington: Indiana University Press, 1988.

————. "Some Enigmas of Chopin's Pedal Indications: What Do the Sources Tell Us?" *Journal of Musicological Research* 16.1 (1996), 41–61.

Rowland, David. *A History of Pianoforte Pedalling*. Cambridge: Cambridge University Press, 1993.

Rubinstein, Anton. *Guide to the Proper Use of the Pianoforte Pedals (with examples out of the Historical Concerts of Anton Rubinstein)*. Leipzig: Bosworth & Co., 1897.

Schmitt, Hans. *The Pedals of the Pianoforte*. Trans. Frederick S. Law. Philadelphia: Theodore Presser, 1893.

Schnabel, Karl Ulrich. *Modern Technique of the Pedal*. Milan: Curci; New York: Mills, 1954.

Shlyapnikov, Vladimir. "The Neglected Left Pedal." *Clavier* 39.6 (2000), 7–11.

APPENDIX C
Works Cited in this Book

Excerpts from the following piano works are included in this book to illustrate the principles of artistic pedal technique.

ACKNOWLEDGEMENTS

Norton, Christopher
Dreaming
Source: *The Microjazz Collection 3*
© Copyright 1983, 1997 by Boosey & Hawkes Music
 Publishers Ltd. Reprinted by permission of Boosey
 & Hawkes, Inc.

Reubart, Dale
Bolero
Source: *Pantomimes*
© Copyright 1996 The Frederick Harris Music Co.,
 Limited, Mississauga, Ontario, Canada. All rights
 reserved.

March of the Buffoons
Source: *Pantomimes*
© Copyright 1996 The Frederick Harris Music Co.,
 Limited, Mississauga, Ontario, Canada. All rights
 reserved.

Szelenyi, Istvan
Faraway Regions
Source: *Musical Picture Book*
© Copyright 1967 Editio Musica Budapest, Hungary.
 Reprinted by permission.

The following works are published in *Celebration Series®*, *The Piano Odyssey®* by The Frederick Harris Music Co., Limited.

Piano Repertoire 2
Bender, Joanne: *Inuit Lullaby*
Szelényi, István: *Faraway Regions*

Piano Repertoire 3
Bartók, Béla: *Play*
Berlin, Boris: *The Haunted Castle*
Fuchs, Robert: *Timid Little Heart*, op. 47,
 no. 5
Henderson, Ruth: *Lullaby in Black and White*
Tchaikovsky, Pyotr Il'yich: *Morning Prayer*,
 op. 39, no. 1

Piano Repertoire 4
Bartók, Béla: *Children's Game*
Benedict, Robert: *Shallows*
Duke, David: *Barcarole*
Weber, Carl Maria von: *Waltz in G Major*,
 op. 4, no. 2

Piano Repertoire 5
Coulthard, Jean: *Star Gazing*
Kuzmenko, Larysa: *Romance*
Norton, Christopher: *Dreaming*
Schumann, Robert: *A Little Romance*, op. 68,
 no. 19

Piano Repertoire 6
Clementi, Muzio: *Sonatina in F Major*, op. 36, no. 4,
 second movement
Creston, Paul: *Pastoral Dance*, op. 24, no. 4
Rebikov, Vladimir Ivanovich: *Miniature Waltz*, op. 10,
 no. 10
Reubart, Dale: *March of the Buffoons*
Schubert, Franz: *Sentimental Waltz*, op. 50,
 no. 13

Piano Repertoire 7
Brahms, Johannes: *Waltz in G sharp Minor*, op. 39,
 no. 3
Chopin, Frédéric: *Prélude in B Minor*, op. 28,
 no. 4
Louie, Alexina: *Shooting Stars*
Rebikov, Vladimir Ivanovich: *Waltz*

Piano Repertoire 8
Chopin, Frédéric: *Prélude in B Minor*, op. 28,
 no. 6
Liszt, Franz: *Consolation No. 1*
Louie, Alexina: *O Moon*
Schumann, Robert: *An Important Event*, op. 15, no. 6

Piano Repertoire 9
Mozart, Wolfgang Amadeus: *Sonata in C Major*,
 K 300, second movement
Scarlatti, Domenico: *Sonata in D Minor*, L 413, K 9
Schubert, Franz: *Impromptu in A flat Major*,
 op. 142, no. 2

PREFACE

My awareness of the importance of thoughtful pedaling and its myriad possibilities began in graduate school where I learned about the principle of ten levels of pedal as taught by the famed Russian pianist Rosina Lhévinne. When I began teaching college students, I realized that my students were no more knowledgeable about pedaling than I had been in my early training. Convinced that a methodical approach to teaching this area of pianism was important, I looked for some helpful teaching materials but they weren't to be found. I therefore created the exercises and notation that became the basis of this volume. I have found this approach extremely effective in helping my students develop a thoughtful and artistic pedal technique.

I owe thanks to many people for their help in bringing this volume into being. First of all, I wish to thank my dear friend and colleague Seymour Bernstein for his valuable advice, encouragement, and support. In addition, there were so many others who helped me along the way that I cannot name them all. But I would like to give special thanks to the following colleagues and friends for the generous time and expertise they gave to the manuscript and the many revisions: James Callahan, Beatriz Aguerrevere, Jon Iverson, Ann Cader, Carol Flatou. Last but not least I thank my students for their inspiration and all I learned from them.

Katherine Faricy
Minnetonka, Minnesota
2018

Katherine Faricy graduated from the Oberlin College Conservatory of Music with a bachelor's degree in music education and received her master of fine arts degree in piano performance from the University of Minnesota. She also studied privately for four years with the renowned concert pianist, Madame Lili Kraus. As a member of the faculty at the University of St. Thomas in St. Paul, Minnesota, she taught undergraduate piano, piano ensemble, accompanying, and music literature; as well as graduate piano and courses in performance practices, piano literature, and piano pedagogy. A frequent recitalist and soloist with orchestras, Katherine Faricy serves as an adjudicator and clinician. It was during studies with Kraus she became very aware of the importance of pedaling in artistic performance and how few people are taught its technique. *Artistic Pedal Technique—Lessons for Intermediate and Advanced Pianists* was first published in 2004 and has become an international success. In 2009 Faricy's newest book was published, *Pedaling~Colors in Sound; Lessons and Repertoire for Elementary Students*.

Made in the USA
Columbia, SC
30 June 2018